INFLUENTIAL
GARDENERS

INFLUENTIAL GARDENERS

THE DESIGNERS WHO SHAPED 20TH-CENTURY GARDEN STYLE

ANDREW WILSON

CLARKSON POTTER/PUBLISHERS
NEW YORK

For my parents, Edna and Kevin

Published by Clarkson Potter/Publishers,
New York, a division of Random House, Inc.
www.randomhouse.com

Originally published in Great Britain by
Mitchell Beazley, an imprint of Octopus
Publishing Group Ltd, in 2002.

CLARKSON N. POTTER is a trademark
and POTTER and colophon are registered
trademarks of Random House, Inc.

Printed in China

Library of Congress Cataloging-in-Publication
Data is available upon request.

ISBN 1-4000-4811-7

10 9 8 7 6 5 4 3 2 1

First American Edition

Half title page Piet Oudolf's garden, Hummelo,
the Netherlands.
Opposite title page Hestercombe, Somerset, designed
by Gertrude Jekyll and Edwin Lutyens.
Opposite contents page Anthony Paul's garden,
Ockley, Surrey.
Opposite foreword The Odette Monteiro garden,
near Rio de Janeiro, designed by Roberto Burle Marx.

CONTENTS

FOREWORD

"…landscape design may well become total, and may soon supersede architecture as the mother of the arts."

The above statement is from Geoffrey Jellicoe's foreword to *Designing the New Landscape*, Sutherland Lyall's attempt, in the early 1990s, to make sense of contemporary landscape design. Now, after the close of the twentieth century, we have the opportunity to look back upon a period of change and upheaval across the world that, at times, looked desperate and hopeless. Out of this cauldron, landscape and garden design have emerged stronger and more dynamic than before, and certainly more diverse. Although Jellicoe was known first and foremost as a landscape architect, he was also responsible for the development and refinement of garden design as an intellectual endeavour and an art form.

Although this book is inclusive of the many different strands of garden-making, I have to admit that the movement towards art, expression, and pure creativity is both thrilling and rewarding. It is not mutually exclusive of other approaches to the garden, be they plant-led, horticultural, functional, spatial, or architectural; rather, it encompasses all of these and so comes close to Jellicoe's prophecy or hope.

More important, perhaps, the development of a garden puts us in touch with nature, with location or place, and with our individual and collective memories, allowing us to rejuvenate, refresh, and revitalize our lives. As the pace of twentieth-century life constantly quickened, so the garden became more pertinent and valued,

with a true reawakening of interest in the last quarter of the era.

The need for spiritual uplift in our gardens is paramount, and this collection of influential gardens shows this quality above all else. The book is not intended to be encyclopedic and certainly could have included many other talented and accomplished designers. The influence of the gardens and landscapes or of their creators upon both laypeople and professionals has been of primary importance in making this selection. Where possible, influences upon those designers included have also been discussed and identified, expanding and enriching the reference.

What results is a celebration of the best that the twentieth century had to offer in garden and landscape design. In writing the book I have discovered a great deal about this most recent period of history. I have enjoyed researching those designers who are no longer with us, but enjoyed even more the dialogue with those who are very much alive. Their enthusiasm, *joie de vivre*, and sense of humour shines out of every discussion, and I am only sorry that time did not allow me to speak directly to every designer involved.

I would like to take this opportunity to thank many of the designers for their time, interest, and involvement in the development of this project. I would also like to pay tribute to them all for their commitment to their art in all its diversity.

Andrew Wilson

COLOUR & DECORATION

In garden design, two approaches dominated the twentieth century. The designers saw the garden spatially, while decorators saw it as borders to be filled with planting colour and texture. Many decorators developed gardens that already existed, modifying and refining the spaces created by others. Penelope Hobhouse and Christopher Lloyd are in this category. Some designers relied on partners – for example, Gertrude Jekyll on Edwin Lutyens, or Vita Sackville-West on her husband, Harold Nicolson, who was responsible for the more structural planting at Sissinghurst.

Above Mediterranean planting was a favourite of Gertrude Jekyll. At Hestercombe, Somerset, she colour-themed with grey foliage, planting such as stachys and lavender. White, pale pink, and purple-blue were the dominant flower colours.

Opposite The hot borders at Hidcote Manor, Gloucestershire, use the intense flower colour of dahlia, canna, and hemerocallis, mixed with the spiky grasses cordyline and phormium. The purple foliage lends depth to the association.

Previous pages Hidcote Manor, designed by Lawrence Johnston.

officially recognized as a weed and a threat to the stability of some natural habitats. The infamous Japanese knotweed (*Polygonum japonicum*), brought originally to the West as a decorative plant, is almost impossible to eradicate. But although some introductions were failures, the vast majority became part of the fashionable garden scene in western Europe and North America.

Out of this mêlée of plant material, often used to elaborately embellish the Victorian garden, emerged the herbaceous and mixed borders – systems of organizing planting intended to impose some sense of order. William Robinson was a prime mover in this development, condemning at every opportunity the formal excesses of his garden-making contemporaries.

Gertrude Jekyll was greatly influenced by Robinson, a prolific writer who used the media to promote his message of more naturalistic planting. She put many of his ideas into practice in her borders and plantations, sharing and developing the concept of compatible plant associations.

Drawing on her artistic training, Jekyll also experimented with colour, using principles of advancing (warm reds and oranges) and receding (cool blues and purples) hues to accentuate border length and the sense of distance. She relied on the work of Michel Eugène Chevreul, a French chemist researching the qualities of dyes who published his findings to critical acclaim.

Both Robinson and Jekyll dominated the design scene in Britain at a time when the Arts and Crafts Movement was gaining ground. This was essentially a rebellion against manufacture and mass production in favour of the protection of crafts and the traditional skill base of the countryside. Jekyll was accomplished in many arts and decorative skills, but, as a woman of means, she could never have earned a living from such work and would never have been regarded as a professional gardener. *Country Life*, a journal dedicated to the promotion and protection of Britain's rural life, was launched towards the end of the nineteenth century, and Jekyll was a regular contributor, divulging her gardening secrets to an eager audience.

As the twentieth century dawned the garden was dominated by plantsmanship and horticultural endeavour. For many, this was, and still remains, the whole point of creating a garden.

During the Victorian and Edwardian periods there was an enormous growth in planting interest. It was the era of the intrepid plant hunter, boasting characters such as Reginald Farrer and Ernest "Chinese" Wilson, the latter responsible for the introduction of many garden favourites, including *Lilium regale*, more than sixty rhododendrons, and various flowering cherries. The wealthy and privileged garden owners of the time loved the novelty of these discoveries, filling their gardens with new and unusual plants and, in doing so, introducing the odd pernicious weed.

In parts of Britain the common *Rhododendron ponticum*, planted originally for game cover, is now

Above At Cruden Farm, Victoria, Australia, Edna Walling's use of colour-themed borders of the kind seen all over England revealed the Jekyllian influences that shaped her early approach. This theming and display of flowers evolved into an international phenomenon derived from the English garden style, becoming the template for millions of gardeners.

continental Europe, the garden became most influential in Britain in the early twentieth century amid Arts and Crafts fever. The industrial age had produced a new rich stratum in society: people who were keen to acquire the lifestyle and values of the more established gentry. The lifestyle garden lived on in Britain through most of the twentieth century, indicative of social class and status.

The houses and gardens of Lutyens, for example, fitted the need perfectly. The concept of the colour border and the decorative use of plants established by Jekyll in response to these gardens was to echo through the century. Visually, Lutyens' gardens were stunning, rich in variety and alive with exciting plant combinations, maintained by artifice and a huge input of labour.

The borders were often created purely for display, on the pattern of lowest planting to the fore and tallest to the rear. This is evident in much of the planting at Sissinghurst, Kent – perhaps the most famous of all British gardens – renowned above all else for its decorative planting. Vita Sackville-West lived for her planting there, writing about it in *The Observer* to popular acclaim, and refining her ideas in the process.

These flower-dominated gardens used the device of compartments, often created in hedges of yew, hornbeam, or holly. Lawrence Johnston exemplified this approach at Hidcote Manor, Gloucestershire, with a fascinating sequence of spaces created partially at least to house his burgeoning collection of plants from all over the world. The hedges effectively provide consistency to an otherwise disparate collection.

In Britain there existed something of a mutual admiration society, with many of these gardeners visiting one another's gardens and sharing their experiences. Their influence eventually spread abroad, extending to Beatrix Farrand in North America, and later to Lanning Roper, an American living in England, and Edna Walling in Australia. The romance of these gardens struck a chord with many, and the decorative manipulation of planting as the *raison d'être* of the garden was established, becoming a dominant strand in the making of gardens throughout the world.

The National Trust was also founded during this period to save, in Britain's national interest, the heritage endangered by the aristocracy diminishing in importance and wealth. The Trust became the saviour of artistic endeavour and the world's largest garden owner, ensuring at the same time that the British would cling to the past for most of the following century.

Ironically, what started as a rebellion against formality and indulgence, taking reference from the cottage-garden planting of the English county of Surrey, became an intensively supported indulgence, contained within a semi-Italianate framework built on the back of cheap labour.

Although what is known as the Modern Movement or modernism was establishing itself in

The garden historian Jane Brown refers to these early twentieth-century creations as "gardens of a golden afternoon" because many were linked to the rich and aristocratic society of the first half of the century. After the Second World War, sweeping social changes made such gardens unsustainable, yet their romance lived on.

It took more than a half-century for women to be accepted as professionals in a field in which the amateur is still fêted. Rosemary Verey and Penelope Hobhouse, two of the most influential flower gardeners of all time, continued the decorative strand of garden-making in a resurgence of interest after the 1966 publication of Jekyll's biography by Betty Massingham. Just as the cottage garden had received a romantic make-over from Jekyll, so in turn the decorative flower borders of late twentieth-century gardens were transformed into rich tapestries of colourful and luxuriant planting. Often Verey and Hobhouse worked within an existing design framework to apply their planting magic to the borders. Where such frameworks did not exist, new gardens maintained an axial or formal approach, with controlled views and vistas created by means of hedges. The gardens succeed through their luxuriant colour planting, which overlays or softens the underlying or formative structure.

Although working in a different vein, Christopher Lloyd employs the same philosophy, approaching the planting of a border as an artist would approach a painting. He plays with colour, experimenting endlessly and usually providing a glorious feast for the eye. In his garden at Great Dixter, East Sussex, the structure is already set, with the planting providing a changing tableau from one year to the next.

Many of these plantsmen and plantswomen have used the pen to spread their word. Besides her articles for *Country Life*, Jekyll wrote books explaining her thinking. Verey, Hobhouse, and Lloyd have all done likewise, producing best-selling publications, while Lloyd also followed in Sackville-West's footsteps as a garden columnist.

In many ways it is the writing that has been responsible for the success of this style, with newspaper editors and publishers keen to promote this visually stimulating and photogenic concept. The maintenance of these decorative borders is a demanding task, and the continuing attention to detail is phenomenal. As society continued to change and develop, and time became an increasingly precious resource, these gardens began to wane in popularity for all except those with time and money on their hands.

The herbaceous border is undoubtedly a triumph of the twentieth century. Although John Claudius Loudon promoted this approach to planting as early as 1840, it was Jekyll who perfected the full flowering of this garden feature. Towards the end of the twentieth century plantsmanship managed to circumvent modernism and achieve a renaissance in the hands of Verey and Hobhouse, whose decorative creations will glow with evocative beauty for many years to come.

Below Penelope Hobhouse is the current successor to the tradition established by Gertrude Jekyll, creating intense, exciting, colour combinations in decorative planting design. Often working within an existing framework, as here at Tintinhull House, Somerset, she transforms and softens the character and atmosphere of gardens with her romantic touch.

Gertrude Jekyll

"To plant and maintain a flower border, with a good scheme for colour, is by no means the easy thing that is commonly supposed."

Gertrude Jekyll

It may well be that the title of most influential garden designer should be granted to Gertrude Jekyll (1843–1932), although this honour must be shared with Edwin Lutyens, with whom Jekyll formed one of the discipline's most productive partnerships. Together they dominated the dawn of the twentieth century, producing designs that would influence garden-making right into the present century. Most important, Jekyll was also a prolific writer, spreading her word through many books and the journal *Country Life*.

Jekyll's upbringing was liberal, and her interest in art led her to the Kensington School of Art, an

unusual step for a woman in Victorian society. She later went to Greece, Crete, and Rhodes, which opened her eyes to a world of planting outside Surrey. Socially, she was introduced to John Ruskin, William Morris, and Edward Burne-Jones, and was well aware of their emerging Arts and Crafts Movement. She added embroidery and metalwork to her artistic skills, producing work worthy of exhibition. For a woman of private means, however, it would have been impossible to make the leap from gifted amateur to professional artist. To have been paid for her work would have been unacceptable, and she had to content herself with exchanging views on the nature of light and colour with the artist Hercules Brabazon Brabazon, although this influenced her later planting designs.

Jekyll's early love of gardens and plants came to her rescue as her eyesight began to fail in her

Left The gardens at Munstead Wood provided Jekyll with a trial ground for her colour theories and planting associations. This prewar photograph shows the profusion in her wide flower borders, into which potted specimens were inserted to prolong the seasonal effect.

15

Choisya · Cistus cyprius · Piptanthus · Carpenteria · Abutilon vitifolium · Loquat

Yucca · White Holly · Yucca · Sulphur Hollyhocks · Clem. Jackm. · Echinops · Symb. latif. · White Dahlia

Seakwort · Echinops · White Dahlia · Aster umbellatus · Aster Shorts · Yucca

Elymus · Tall yellow Snapdra · Achillea · Campanula lactiflora

Hydrangea · Snapdragon · Dictam · Hydrangea · Geranium ibericum · Aster acris · Rue · Yucca filam

Yucca filam · Seakal · Cineraria maritima · Santolina · Cineraria maritima

Stachys

Yew. Arbour under

Above In this plan of part of the Long Border at Munstead Wood, the pattern of Jekyll's planting is evident. Drifts of plants overlapped and wove together in order to create a seamless sequence and to hide plants that were past their seasonal prime.

Opposite Although Lutyens was responsible for the hard structure of their gardens, Jekyll's planting decisions played a key role. At Hestercombe, Somerset, the stone and tile steps are invaded by *Cerastium tomentosum* and the somewhat more imposing euphorbia to create a successful yet still unusual fusion between architect and garden designer.

thirties, through myopia. Her photographic work includes mainly details and close-up imagery, perhaps indicating the limitations of her sight. The fine work involved in her art and craft became increasingly difficult, but the scale of the garden canvas was much more tangible and rewarding.

William Robinson had already made a significant impact on gardening sensibility with his first book, *The Wild Garden*, published in 1870. Jekyll came to know him well, contributing to his journal, *The Garden*. Those with Arts and Crafts leanings warmed to his naturalistic message, which would influence garden design for over a century. Jekyll and Robinson probably discussed the content of his second book, *The English Flower Garden*, and it is possible that ideas framed here were actually hers although attributed to Robinson.

Eventually Jekyll bought the 6ha (15 acres) of land in Surrey that became Munstead Wood, and at this point, in search of an architect, she met Edwin Lutyens, thus starting an extremely productive and lasting partnership. At first Lutyens learned from her about both house and garden, but their relationship soon developed into a balanced partnership, despite his being twenty years younger.

Jekyll had the social contacts that Lutyens needed to enhance his career, but in effect he became her eyes, paying attention to detail and creating the structural backbone of their gardens through paving, construction, and architecture. They would visit sites together, Lutyens dealing with the layout, often discussed over tea or supper, and Jekyll applying her skill to the planting design.

Using Michel Eugène Chevreul's *The Principles of Harmony and Contrast of Colours and their Application to the Arts*, Jekyll applied colour theory to her large-scale borders. Chevreul's theories were

appropriate to planting, covering harmonies, contrasts, and colour triads. Jekyll's borders became famous, through her writing, her work at Munstead Wood, and her collaboration with Lutyens.

Their schemes were not for the faint-hearted. The main border at Munstead Wood measured 70m (230ft) by 4m (13ft) and at one time Jekyll employed seventeen gardeners. The border was designed to start flowering in July and fade in October – she had a policy of applying seasonal effects to different parts of the garden. In essence, she took her ideas from the cottage gardens she saw near her home and applied them on a grand scale and in carefully ordered colour sequences. In addition she used Mediterranean plants to good effect in the dry, sandy soil of west Surrey.

Although Jekyll worked for other architects and produced gardens in her own right, all of her best gardens were produced in collaboration with Lutyens. For this reason she could be described as a decorator, but she nevertheless had a firm grip on spatial design and always talked of her plants in connection with specific locations and in terms of three dimensions. "Show me your spaces and I will tell you what plants to get for them," she wrote in the journal *House & Garden* in 1900.

Jekyll's drifts of inspired colour planting have influenced many, not least through a renewal of interest, towards the end of the twentieth century, that brought her to a new generation of gardeners and designers. For this we must thank in part Beatrix Farrand, who rescued Jekyll's planting plans and supporting notes from destruction, and disseminated her ideas to an American audience.

After Jekyll's death, few garden owners were able to afford such expansive schemes, although Millmead, a narrow plot in Bramley, Surrey, was a prominent forerunner of many suburban gardens, reaching the masses through coverage in her book *Gardens for Small Country Houses*. Many of Jekyll's planting schemes have been lost, too fragile to survive the rigours of a demanding and revolutionary century. Although some have been recreated, most of her schemes live on in the Reef Point Collection, in California – a hotbed of garden-making of a very different kind.

Vita Sackville-West

"Fortunate gardener, who may preoccupy himself solely with beauty…
A useless member of society, considered in terms of economics, he must
not be denied his rightful place. He deserves to share it, however
humbly, with the painter and the poet."

Vita Sackville-West

Vita Sackville-West (1892–1962) is primarily responsible for what has become arguably the most famous garden in the world, Sissinghurst Castle, Kent. Renowned internationally as a perfect example of the English garden, it receives thousands of visitors every year.

Sackville-West spent her early life at Knole House, also in Kent. As a child she enjoyed the beautiful gardens that formed the immediate estate and penetrated its inner courtyards.

Left The view from the tower at Sissinghurst demonstrates the relationship between the structural walls and hedges and the luxuriant, decorative planting. This contrast between the formality of lawn and hedge and looser, organic forms epitomizes the English garden style.

In 1913 she married Harold Nicolson in the chapel at Knole, and the couple's first home was nearby Long Barn, a combination of a rustic cottage and a re-erected barn. The garden was ripe for development, and Sackville-West started to plant the new terraces and borders defined by the L-shaped house. From the start her interest lay in creating associations of colour and texture that pleased the eye and delighted the senses. Harold was more keen to establish a framework – the underlying architecture of the garden.

Edwin Lutyens was certainly involved in the planning of parts of the garden at Long Barn, particularly the Dutch garden, which was paid for by Sackville-West's mother. Lady Sackville also

provided the majority of plants with which her daughter stocked the borders, and introduced her to Gertrude Jekyll at Munstead Wood, Jekyll's home in Surrey. This convergence of design influences increased Sackville-West's confidence with planting. It would seem that, without Long Barn, Sissinghurst would not have been possible.

Harold and Vita acquired Sissinghurst Castle, the remnant of an Elizabethan house, in 1930. Its collection of buildings gradually became a home suitable for this hopelessly romantic family. By now both were successful writers, and they used the income from their work to pursue their developing interest in their garden.

Although Sackville-West was acclaimed as a poet, she gained wider recognition through her garden writing for *The Observer* between 1946 and 1962 and through the success of Sissinghurst. She

had the ability to describe her approach to gardening, notably planting, in familiar, comfortable language that was never condescending but always full of interest and enthusiasm.

Early on at Sissinghurst, large-scale clearance of dereliction was needed to reveal the hidden structure. Planting, started in the early 1930s, was a combination of existing elements, such as the nut walk, and new borders, along with climbers selected for the walls, and hedges introduced to form new enclosures. In time this developed into the exuberant yet always carefully analyzed planting that became Sissinghurst's trademark.

William Robinson provided inspiration here, and Sackville-West visited him at nearby Gravetye Manor, where he would show off his garden. The original planting beneath the nut walk is thought to have been a tribute to Robinson, whose books she valued. The architect Albert Powys frequently worked as a consultant at Sissinghurst, although Sackville-West always insisted that she and her husband had developed the garden alone.

As the Second World War approached, Sackville-West dedicated more time to her garden, which began to attract visitors and was opened to the public in 1938 under the National Gardens Scheme. In the decades after the war the stream of visitors, including a growing number from overseas, continued to swell.

More famous than the whole conglomeration was the White Garden, created after Sackville-West observed the luminous qualities of white flowers in the fading light of dusk. The planting was developed in the late 1940s and has remained a tribute to her skill. The idea has been copied around the world, perpetuating a craze for colour-themed planting, and it has surely inspired both Penelope Hobhouse and Rosemary Verey.

Sackville-West did not want to hand over Sissinghurst to the National Trust, having been critical of its tendency to preserve the old and ignore the new. Nevertheless, the organization assumed responsibility for the garden in 1967, and has proved to be its saviour. And while much has changed, the guiding spirit of Vita Sackville-West still seems to linger there.

Rosemary Verey

"Good bones are important, so it is wise to go slowly and get your plan right before launching into a vital project."

Rosemary Verey

Rosemary Verey (1918–2001), who, sadly, died during the writing of this book, was a phenomenon of twentieth-century gardening history, representing the potential of older women coming into garden-making as a second career. She could have lived quietly in the country, but ended her career jetting around the world to deliver lectures, creating gardens for pop stars and princes, and writing best-selling books.

In her youth she read economics at University College London, but her professional ambitions took second place to her family responsibilities. In the early twentieth century this was the anticipated

Left Barnsley House was Verey's signature garden, a sequence of decorative tableaux arranged around her home in the Cotswolds. In using the building as a backdrop for her decorative planting compositions, she was well aware of the value of structure.

role for women, for whom education might open doors but marriage would curtail exploration.

Verey's husband, David, was an architectural historian who fired her with an interest in garden history. In addition, she was a good tennis player and enjoyed hunting, introducing her children to horse riding, and at that time using the garden of David's parental home, Barnsley House, Gloucestershire, very much as a playground.

As Verey reached middle age, her husband urged her to return the garden's grassed-over borders to their former glory, and so her career began. At first it was the substantial stone house itself, with its mature trees, hedges, and a strong atmosphere, that fascinated her most. However, spurred on by the gift of a gardening diary, she began to take an interest in plants, visiting shows at the Royal Horticultural Society in London. Her confidence and her knowledge of plants grew, and in 1960 she started to expand the structure and ornamentation of the garden at Barnsley House.

This garden follows formal and symmetrical rules, with the main section taking its layout from the elevation of the seventeenth-century building. Verey used Russell Page's *The Education of a Gardener* as her bible, taking heart from his structured approach, and learning to create strong axes and visual routes through the garden. Many visitors find this garden much smaller than they imagined. It must be one of the most photographed compositions in the history of garden-making, but the camera can provide a misleading sense of scale.

Verey's fame followed the development of the garden and its opening to the public. Its immense popularity paid homage to an amazing work of decorative plantsmanship. The Vereys introduced follies to create focal points. The borders between these were filled with colour-schemed flowering perennials and shrubs, knot gardens, box-trimmed associations, and, to crown it all – though on a much smaller scale than its famous counterpart at Bodnant, North Wales – a laburnum tunnel, underplanted with allium, hosta, and white digitalis. Frothy alchemilla bounded through the garden, seeding its sulphur-yellow lacework above downy, dew-covered leaves. The age of flower gardening had matured, a romanticization of the ideas of Gertrude Jekyll and Vita Sackville-West.

The result was a garden photographer's dream: images of glorious colour and sumptuous texture available at almost every turn, disseminated around the world in a series of richly illustrated books or captured on film. It is therefore the fame of Barnsley House that projected Verey onto the international stage. By her own admission she was not a designer, yet her advice on garden design was in great demand. Her interests continued to be planting, a range of successful experiments (moving plants around, developing a potager, maintaining existing associations), and writing. Verey's books greatly increased her popularity, with *The Making of a Garden* providing insight into the development of Barnsley House, and *The American Woman's Garden* contributing to her widespread acceptance in the United States.

Some of this astounding fame was attributed by Verey to the humble but curious mandrake, which so fascinated her when, early on, she came across a stray paper entitled "The Insane Root" among her husband's books. Without this glimpse into history, perhaps little out of the ordinary would have happened in Verey's life. As it was, she struck a note of popularity, just as Sackville-West had managed to communicate widely with her column in *The Observer* twenty years earlier.

Verey's fame and ascendancy coincided with the expansion of leisure time and personal wealth that distinguished the twentieth century from its precursors. Many more individuals had time on their hands, money to spend or invest, properties in their care, and a media keen to tell them what to do with all of these. In Britain, Verey was the perfect symbol of the gifted amateur, capable of achieving a level of excellence that was still seen as worthy; to readers in other countries her work represented the quintessential English style, and borders throughout the world came to be filled with Vereyesque planting.

Although she was, to some extent, surprised by this popularity, Verey did not allow it to affect either her judgment or her approachability. She was always happy to be on hand at Barnsley House, providing visitors with information and advice, which she dispensed with humour and wit. She was certainly of great help to Penelope Hobhouse, whom she encouraged in practical garden-making, planting, and lecturing.

It is easy to speculate that, given a different set of circumstances, not least a house without a history and the lack of a historian husband, Verey might never have become the consummate plantswoman that she was. However, she attacked her new career with great vigour and enthusiasm, creating one of the most influential gardens of the twentieth century. She represented no particular movement and had received no training in design or horticulture, yet she conveyed a message to millions: that they too could expand their planting knowledge and create special gardens.

Penelope Hobhouse

"Even the most irresistible flowering plant, one that I call a 'key' performer, is part of a whole cast; it has to be considered as a component in an overall look as well as for its individual charms."

Penelope Hobhouse

The closing decades of the twentieth century were dominated by the flower garden – sequences of richly varied plant associations developed within the structured framework of the traditional English garden. Penelope Hobhouse (b.1929) epitomizes this genre. Encouraged by Rosemary Verey, Hobhouse now stands alongside her mentor as a dominant name in flower gardening.

Hobhouse's first book, *Colour in Your Garden*, published in 1985, was an instant success as it combined science and art in an approachable way. *Flower Gardens* (1991) was more sophisticated,

Left This rich interplanting at Hadspen House is typical of Hobhouse's decorative style. Her borders are densely packed with carefully co-ordinated colour and texture, and are high on visual impact. Here, upright grasses nestle beneath the spreading architectural foliage of angelica.

dealing with the decorative approach to planting design and successful plant association. Islamic and Renaissance gardens are especially important to Hobhouse, and she identifies her main influences as Russell Page, Sylvia Crowe, and Christopher Lloyd.

In a period when progressive design should have been prevalent, Hobhouse's retrospective work found immense popularity, supported by her highly successful lecture tours across the world. There is certainly artistry in the flower garden, although this is mainly confined to the border rather than the structured layout. Ravishing photographs of associations, with flower and foliage spilling over paths or clambering over rustic walls and clipped yew, sold a complex concept to an eager audience.

Inundated with requests for design advice, Hobhouse rose to the challenge with enthusiasm.

Above left Plant-dominated gardens such as Tintinhull House are typical of Hobhouse's approach, in which subtle blends of colour and texture provide a romantic and classically English quality. The underlying geometry is invariably formal.

Above right Although foliage is important in Hobhouse's work, it is the ravishing flower colour that is her most potent tool. Stands of single plants, such as these irises at Tintinhull House, are often contrasted with intricate colour associations.

Opposite The large country garden in which Hobhouse specializes is a perfect vehicle for her soft, plant-rich borders. The flower-garden style, seen here in a private garden in France, was made popular by her books and has been imitated all over the world.

She has grown in stature as both designer and plantswoman, and continues to create increasingly ambitious and beautifully planted gardens. The one she designed in Detroit is particularly precious to her and is a well-maintained example of her work.

Gertrude Jekyll, through whom she learned about the application of colour theory to the herbaceous border, was another major influence. Subsequently Hobhouse studied the French Impressionist painters, well aware of the close relationship of their colour theories to the way in which planting colour works. She was especially interested in Chevreul and Monet, whose work with colour has proved so inspirational to gardeners.

Hobhouse is synonymous with the gardens of Tintinhull House and Hadspen House, both in Somerset. These were existing gardens, which, when touched by her magic, became places of pilgrimage. Tintinhull was originally a farmhouse, albeit one with grand aspirations. Its garden was given an Arts and Crafts make-over to create a series of "rooms," originally planted by Phyllis Reiss, who acquired the house in 1933. The property was later given to the National Trust.

As the tenant of Hadspen House from 1980 to 1993, Hobhouse developed the gardens by planting the borders with rich associations and

restoring the earlier structure. She transformed them into a series of tableaux based on colour effects separated by yew hedges. This fondness for hedged structure, against which planting takes place, has led to Hobhouse being regarded as a traditionalist – an approach that has been a key element of all her gardens. The layouts are usually axial and symmetrical, with the main interest focused on the intensity of plant combinations.

Hobhouse remains popular with plantsmen and plantswomen, as her style of garden-making calls for high maintenance. What is remarkable is the richness of palette used in her associations, with layers of interplanting exploited to extend seasonal interest or to intensify colour experience. In this area she is rightly regarded as influential.

Despite the advent of the "New Perennial" approach to planting design, with its reliance on sustainability and lower maintenance levels, Hobhouse remains the outstanding decorative plantswoman of her generation, part of a seamless continuum running through the twentieth century. In all of her work it is the glory of the planting that dominates and takes pride of place. For this she will be justifiably remembered, her well-documented work and writing providing inspiration for thousands.

Above Although Walling initially championed the English garden in Australia, she gradually came to recognize the value of the landscape and flora of her adopted country. With its entrance avenue of *Eucalyptus citriodora*, Cruden Farm is an early design that prefigures the direction that her later work would take.

Walling's early work was inspired by Gertrude Jekyll, and decorative planting schemes dominated her designs. But whereas Jekyll's plans were mundane and had the quality of working sketches, Walling's were beautifully crafted watercolour explorations of the site, characterized by a distinct three-dimensional quality and an exquisite economy of line and colour.

There was a formal quality to her work, with its Italianate references influenced by Jellicoe and Shepherd's *Italian Gardens of the Renaissance*, published in 1925. But as she settled into the Australian landscape, so its beauty began to weave its magic into her designs. Cruden Farm, Victoria, one of Walling's early gardens, used lemon-scented *Eucalyptus citriodora* to define the main drive. The almost-white trunks create a sensational entrance to the property yet also relate directly to the surrounding landscape.

As Walling matured, her designs became free and loose, softening through a curvilinear progression that left behind a forced Italian formality. This more relaxed approach allowed the planting style to soften too, moving away from the purely decorative colour-based planting to textured, luxuriant undergrowth, out of which the structure of her designs emerged.

Walling came to represent a more modern philosophy, suggesting that her whole outlook on the basic purpose of a garden had changed, to a place in which to relax rather than work. Alongside her garden design work, she contributed regularly to *Australian Home Beautiful*, often showing her plans to make her point. She became a popular figure in horticultural circles and beyond, her enthusiasm for garden-making always infectious. Markdale, New South Wales, and Greenacres, in Hobart, Tasmania, are two of Walling's most ambitious and memorable gardens, carefully structured and large enough to contain a varied sequence of spaces, although many of her gems are hidden in the suburbs of Australia's major cities.

Based near Melbourne, and inspired by a growing passion for Australia's landscape, Walling took a "hands-off" approach that hinted at an early awareness of environmental issues.

Edna Walling

One of Australia's most prolific garden designers, Edna Walling (1896–1973) continued working almost until the end of her life. She was a lady of great character, originating from Yorkshire, England, and was a member of one of the many British families who emigrated to New Zealand but later settled in Australia.

At first she loathed gardens, feeling that she had been presented with a *fait accompli* when her mother decided that a schooling in horticulture would suit her very well. The manual labour required to maintain gardens was an anathema to her until she realized that the three-dimensional architecture of those in which she worked in fact captured her imagination.

Christopher Lloyd

Christopher Lloyd (b.1921) is inseparable from his garden at Great Dixter, East Sussex. He has dedicated most of his life to its development, and much of his writing, for which he is rightly famous, stems from his continuing work in this beautiful garden. Edwin Lutyens extended the old house at Dixter, parts of which date back to 1464, and with the addition came the original layout for the garden. The sunken water garden was designed and built by Nathanial Lloyd, who also planted yew-hedged compartments to replace the walls suggested by Lutyens.

The excitement offered by the garden at Great Dixter lies mainly in Lloyd's willingness to experiment and to enjoy the fun of gardening, including the mistakes that occasionally result from this approach. Always interesting, the garden combines the best of wild-flower meadows and exotic planting.

The garden is still in flux, with the planting providing an ever-changing tableau. Now in his eighties, Lloyd retains an undiminished passion for planting. Indeed the recent replacement of the old rose garden with an exuberant association of exotics showed a gardener willing to develop new ideas. This constant state of evolution is the result of a close and successful partnership between Lloyd and his head gardener, Fergus Garrett.

Lloyd, who studied horticulture and later taught at Wye College, has written some twenty books, many based on his experiences at Great Dixter and widely acclaimed for the candid views they express. Perhaps the most famous is *The Well-Tempered Garden*, first published in 1970. Lloyd reaches an even wider audience through his regular columns in *The Guardian* and *Country Life*, contributing to the latter every week since 1963. The gardening feeds the writing, which in turn provides a vehicle for reflecting on new ideas. Since 1950 many thousands of readers have benefited from Lloyd's insights into the complex interrelationships that lie at the heart of planting design.

Below At Great Dixter, Lloyd experiments enthusiastically with plant associations, producing a different design emphasis each year. These changing tableaux are set against the clipped yew hedges that give the garden its character. This approach works in tandem with Lloyd's extensive writing, which has influenced a generation of gardeners throughout the world.

PLANTING

For many, planting is the whole point of the garden, although there is confusion over the difference between plant collecting and planting design. The former is a hangover from the Victorians, who saw plants as trophies. The latter developed further in the twentieth century as designers began to use plants to enhance atmosphere, create sculptural impact, and intensify emotional or artistic qualities. The concept of plant association developed, combining aesthetic, horticultural, and ecological principles with an emphasis on sustainability as the century closed.

William Robinson detested this sense of control in overall design terms and also found the ordering of plants in systematic rows and patterns quite distasteful. In the late nineteenth century his writing was provocatively preaching a different sermon. He was interested in the plants themselves and the habitats from which they came. In this he was supported and encouraged by Gertrude Jekyll, who had taken the trouble to introduce herself after reading his first book, *The Wild Garden*, published in 1870. This promoted the planting of hardy exotics in conditions that closely resembled their original growing conditions. The title suggested something much more native in quality, but the intention of the writing was to create a sense of habitat in which a variety of species, whether indigenous or not, would create a successful and mutually supportive community.

This revolutionary approach was both typically English in its apparently soft and casual manner and avant-garde in the extreme, predating the innovative planting techniques of the New Perennial Movement by almost a century. The relaxed style, which belied a great deal of research, observation, and skill, set the scene for planting to be the dominant consideration in garden design for almost one hundred years.

Interestingly, Robinson was one of the first garden designers or plantsmen to understand the need to communicate to a wider market than one's own clients. He wrote extensively in journals, and also published some of his own. His books still adorn domestic bookshelves and libraries across the world, running into many editions. He created or advised on fewer gardens than Reginald Blomfield yet managed to influence a century of plantsmen and plantswomen.

Apart from Jekyll, Robinson had a crowd of eager disciples, one of the most devoted of whom was the American Beatrix Farrand. She was an Anglophile, who travelled widely, meeting Jekyll, whose drawings and notebooks she was later to save for posterity, and corresponding with Robinson on a regular basis. Whereas Jekyll was to be distracted by her precious colour theories and partnership with the often formalistic Edwin

Above William Robinson was the gardener who was primarily responsible for the move towards plantsmanship, an approach that was to dominate the twentieth century. The luxuriant and informal planting at Gravetye Manor, in East Sussex, is typical of this trend.

Previous pages Piet Oudolf's own garden at Hummelo, near Arnhem, in the Netherlands. The brightly-coloured herbaceous perennials and grasses typify his planting designs..

The twentieth century opened with a battle royal between the formalists, championed by Sir Reginald Blomfield, and the naturalistic school, led by William Robinson. The former promoted an architectural concept that was reliant on symmetry and axial layouts, and is often described as the Beaux-Arts approach. The École des Beaux-Arts, in Paris, taught design inspired by classical French solutions of the seventeenth and eighteenth centuries. The teaching was widely accepted in the West and was particularly prevalent in the United States, still reinforcing the fundamental principles against which the garden designers Garrett Eckbo, James Rose, and Dan Kiley were to revolt in the 1930s.

Lutyens, Farrand, transported many of Robinson's ideas across the Atlantic and structured her gardens with plants. She had a feel for the context of her gardens and was able to apply the Robinsonian approach to planting associations without being formulaic. She even returned to her source and provided sensitive planting for the visionary community that Leonard and Dorothy Elmhirst were developing in Dartington, Devon.

Another designer to be influenced by Jekyll and Robinson was Mien Ruys. In the early years of the twentieth century women were eager to work as garden designers but in many cases were unable to practise as professionals because of their social class. Jekyll was something of a pioneer in studying at art college when she had a private income as an upper-middle-class lady.

Farrand toyed with the idea of training formally but found it difficult to penetrate what was still a male-dominated world. Ruys managed to train in both educational and practical terms,

eventually turning a burning ambition and passion into a successful career. She is a major link between the plant-orientated gardening of Britain, the horticultural traditions of the Netherlands, and the modernism of the wider continent of Europe. "Although she liked to acknowledge the influence of Gertrude Jekyll and William Robinson on her planting design, their styles were often overlaid with her instinctive empathy with the Dutch modernists," Jane Brown wrote in *The Modern Garden*. Ruys embodied a love of plants but with a selective and artistic use of plant material that the British find difficult even as the twenty-first century begins.

Ruys was interested in the individual forms of the plants she used rather than in seeing plants as a single mass of decorative elements. She would use clipped forms of box, yew, or hornbeam to contrast with free and organic planting structure, setting severe horizontal hedges against soaring vertical stems. In short, she sculpted with plants,

Below Mien Ruys was one of the first trained women garden designers to compete successfully in a male-dominated discipline. In her garden at Dedemsvaart, the simple power of her modernist palette, emphasizing the sculptural form of the plants, contrasts with the English tradition of over-stuffed borders.

Above *Allium christophii* and *Lavandula stoechas* var. *pedunculata* enjoy the dry conditions of Beth Chatto's gravel garden. Truly in tune with the needs of her plants, she adopted an ecological approach that chimed with the late twentieth century's call for sustainability. Her work has inspired a generation of gardeners and garden designers.

to run to the very door of his client's property. Modernists are often still condemned for their lack of sensitivity to planting when in fact they were simply selective with the material they chose to use. Plants were selected for their sculptural presence, occupying space and introducing drama. Hosta, fatsia, acanthus, ferns, and bamboo were often used for their textures and architectural qualities. Perhaps it was as a reaction to these more spartan and minimalist qualities, influenced by Japanese and Scandinavian design and still prevalent in the 1950s, that the English flower garden seized the imagination of the masses, providing a romantic escape from a restrained and sometimes grey world.

Elsewhere, naturalistic concepts in planting design were taking shape, and here there is an interesting interplay between the United States and Europe. Planting in continental Europe has always been more naturalistic in approach, linking in part with the earlier writing of William Robinson. This often ecological philosophy in turn influenced designers such as Jens Jensen, who himself had European roots. In partnership with Frank Lloyd Wright, Jensen developed a response to the American prairie landscape – a phenomenon that had struck a chord through its stunning displays of flowers and grasses, a whole ecosystem playing out dramatically around his adopted city of Chicago. Now, over fifty years later, Wolfgang Oehme and James van Sweden still integrate Euro-American thinking in rich landscapes and gardens inspired by prairies and meadows.

Beth Chatto also promotes this approach, originally gardening as an innocent before being introduced to the complexities of habitat creation by her late husband, an ecologist. She still admits to her sense of wonder at witnessing the breathtaking beauty of the European Alps in flower, a sustainable habitat that puts many endeavours in the garden to shame.

Chatto took the trouble to study both which plants worked best in each area of her garden near Elmstead Market, Essex, and which associations thrived and under what circumstances – art and science mixed. She supported her garden with a

creating rich and atmospheric spaces in her model gardens for the family nursery in Dedemsvaart. She was particularly adept in the use of herbaceous perennials, notably for their form and texture rather than for their flower colour, which again set her apart from her more decoration-conscious counterparts in Britain. This was echoed in the work of Karl Foerster, a champion of herbaceous plants and had considerable influence over many German and Dutch designers and nurserymen.

With the growth of modernism, planting seemed to take a back seat. Built architectural form was often expressed against a natural landscape, reminiscent of those of Lancelot "Capability" Brown, who allowed his landscapes small nursery that specialized in unusual plants and was another gardener who wrote extensively about her experiences, encouraged in this by Graham Stuart Thomas. When the now world-famous planting designer Piet Oudolf was embarking on his career, he visited Chatto's garden and nursery, using it as a model for his own successful venture at Hummelo, in the Netherlands.

Although Oudolf's planting style is rich in colour, and dominated by the softening effect of grasses, he still pays tribute to the influence of Mien Ruys, one of the few designers to understand the qualities of plants as individuals. His use of bold textures and soft drifts against clipped hedges and topiary is reminiscent of Ruys's work. "By seeking to base planting design on structure, it will become apparent that there is something more essential to the soul of plants than colour," he explained in his book *Designing with Plants*.

Dan Pearson also uses grasses as a signature, softening his textures, colours, and forms to create stunning atmospheric gardens that glow with captured light. Oudolf and Pearson share this trait, which sets their gardens apart in allowing them to capture the wildness of the prairie or meadow in a structured and enhanced way.

The New Perennial approach to planting has influenced this late twentieth-century generation of designers, opening up the understanding of sustainability and environmental awareness. Designers such as the German landscape architect Rosemary Weisse have laid down successful planting and maintenance schemes in Germany's public spaces that have percolated into the private gardens of today as well as into the thinking of our contemporary designers.

As a result, decisions about decorative and artistic planting are now tempered by concern for the environment, both local and international. It is accepted that our gardens can appeal to our senses, while at the same time supporting local wildlife and conserving our precious finite resources, an achievement of which William Robinson would have been proud.

Below At Bury Court, Hampshire, Piet Oudolf has produced some of his finest planting. This large island bed is densely planted as a stand of misty deschampsia, reminiscent of the African plain, and out of this emerge the trunks of *Catalpa bignonioides*. The grass border is interplanted with digitalis and allium.

Mien Ruys

*"All her work displays the assurance of modern design
at its very best."*

Jane Brown

Mien Ruys (1904–98) is perhaps the quietest design voice of the twentieth century, a woman who dedicated her life to the creation of satisfying gardens filled with accomplished planting associations.

She was born into horticulture, the daughter of the owner of the Royal Moerheim Nursery, in Dedemsvaart, in the Netherlands. At first, she worked in the nursery, experimenting with garden-making. Her earliest schemes reflect the naturalistic planting prevalent in Europe, influenced by Karl Foerster. Later she travelled to England to gain experience in garden-making,

working for Wallace and Sons in Kent, and meeting Gertrude Jekyll at her home in Surrey, Munstead Wood. The influence of Ruy's English sojourn can be seen in her main border, made in 1927 at Moerheim and still in existence.

After leaving England, Ruys studied at the Dahlem Botanic Garden in Berlin and then pursued a training in architecture in Delft, in her native country. This allowed her to start a career as a landscape architect, and although her early work was dedicated to the garden, she would eventually carry out larger, public commissions.

In 1943 Ruys joined a group of architects known as De 8 en Opbau, who were concerned with functionalism at the expense of unnecessary ornamentation. Her work became more sculptural and architecturally pure but overlaid with planting that was softer and richer. The meeting of the

Left Ruys was one of the first women to benefit from a formal education in garden design, and this enabled her to be accepted into a male world. At Dedemsvaart she illustrated the affinity between architectural hedges and bold masses of softer perennial planting.

Dutch and English schools of thought won her many admirers, and her planting philosophy had a marked impact on many later designers.

Her main contribution to design lay in the sequence of model gardens that she created for the Royal Moerheim Nursery. These were intended to show detailed plant associations and promote sales for the business. Some had a sense of formality, some an air of naturalism, but all demonstrated the harmonious integration of hard and soft materials. Her wild garden was created in 1925, inspired by the development of naturalistic planting in Germany. Sculpture and ornament were often included as focal points, lifting the gardens to a higher plane of artistic endeavour. Anthony Paul, Piet Oudolf, and James van Sweden all see Ruys as inspirational, citing both her public work and her nursery gardens as influential.

The latter are arranged around a central space, and in each area the geometric control is evident through the use of clipped hedges. Such hedges were also used to divide individual borders into smaller blocks, allowing control to be exerted over complex planting groups. Plants were arranged sculpturally, with bold foliage plants used to provide texture and statuesque forms, and vertical spires set against low, horizontal blocks of box.

Ruys seemed content to create her exquisite and carefully considered modern gardens in the Netherlands without resort to the written word. While she undeniably achieved fame in her own country, it was only later that her message spread to designers farther afield. How different gardens in other countries might have looked had she publicized her work more vigorously in the English-speaking world. In 1955, however, she founded the magazine *Onze Eigen Tuin* (*Our Own Garden*), and later produced a book of perennials entitled *Het Nieuwe Vaste Planten Boek* (*The New Perennial Plant Book*). Although both publications were well received, their circulation and their impact on the world of garden design were limited. Nevertheless, it is now clear that Ruys's work has made an outstanding contribution to modern garden and planting design.

Above Ruys exploited the textures of plant material and was one of the first designers to use grasses on a large scale. Access to her father's nursery allowed her to familiarize herself and experiment with a vast range of plants.

Right Although many of the spaces at Dedemsvaart were small, Ruys was expansive in her use of bold drifts and blocks of perennials, influencing many late twentieth-century designers, including Anthony Paul and the partnership of Wolfgang Oehme and James van Sweden.

Beth Chatto

"Designing the garden is like learning to speak. You begin with odd words – learning the individual plants. Then you create a simple phrase, finding two or three plants that look well together, next comes a sentence and finally the complete story."

Beth Chatto

The enthusiam of Beth Chatto (b.1923) for both her garden and her writing gushes out like a spring, full of energy that she seems hardly able to hold back. In fact, Beth has created two gardens – both for herself. The second and the best, near Elmstead Market, Essex, has formed the basis of her writing and has influenced many garden designers, as well as gardeners with a particular interest in plants.

Left The obvious joy in plants shared by Beth Chatto and her late ecologist husband, Andrew, produced the exuberance of her gravel garden. In this part of the garden tall spikes of eremurus and verbascum compete for attention with globes of allium and tissue-like poppies.

Chatto is a native of East Anglia, used to the dry summers and wide skies of this flat area. Her parents owned a small country garden that always interested her, and she learned from them in her early life. At twenty she married Andrew Chatto, of the publishing family of Chatto and Windus, whose interests lay not in publishing but in ecology. Without his influence, she feels, none of her gardening prowess and the writing that followed would have come about.

Beth and Andrew Chatto spent many of their holidays exploring the indigenous flora of the Mediterranean countries and the Alps. Although in the early days Chatto was aware of her lack of

enjoy the same conditions. Chatto's understanding
of this difference marks out her garden as
unusual, if not unique.

Above These dead heads are retained for structural emphasis against strongly vertical but softer masses of ornamental grasses. This creates a textured composition that provides seasonal interest.

Opposite Broad masses of eryngium and anthemis are refreshed by colourful heads of allium and agapanthus. The expanse of texture and colour has a meadow-like quality.

knowledge, she was – and still is – deeply fascinated by these habitats and their planting associations.

Her first garden was on chalky boulder clay, which was difficult to work and very dry. Her visits to the dry regions surrounding the Mediterranean showed the associations that would succeed in this soil and transformed her approach. Chatto's second garden, at White Barn House, also in Essex, has a range of habitats, although she has retained the link with dry gardening with the spectacular gravel garden she created in the old car park.

The garden was developed from a wasteland fed by a natural spring. The soil and source of water appealed immediately to Chatto, who set about clearing both the undergrowth and the planting. She kept most of the existing trees and supplemented them with many others as the flat landscape makes shelter from the wind essential.

Using Andrew as a sounding board, Chatto began to plant species appropriate to their location in the garden, that is to say, creating associations ecologically. Since the 1970s the term "ecological planting" has taken on a new meaning. Originally it was understood to imply native planting, but now it is used to describe plants from a range of different regions, planted together because they

enjoy the same conditions. Chatto's understanding of this difference marks out her garden as unusual, if not unique.

Other influences have affected her approach to planting. One is Cedric Morris, who was introduced to her in the 1950s and became a close friend. She loved to visit his garden, which was planted on a painterly basis, with sheets of flower washing over the beds, regardless of any structural restriction. Another "great," Graham Stuart Thomas, is cited as a major influence, but more through his writing than garden-making. Chatto first met him in Morris's garden, and it was he who suggested that she should write, even recommending her to her future publisher, Dent. Christopher Lloyd is also greatly admired by Chatto, even though they have different approaches.

Chatto sees herself as ploughing her own furrow. Especially since her husband's death, her garden has been a true solace and is still a challenge. She recognizes the need to rethink original ideas but, after forty years, the shelter belts have allowed successful micro-climates to evolve, and Chatto sees many plants as personalities. This sense of isolation is one of the things that makes the garden at White Barn House special. The contrast between the hot and hazy gravel garden and the cool water side and shade planting provides a tremendous sense of change within a relatively small space.

Chatto's writing enables her to reflect on her work and the success of individual associations. She feels that she has become known for growing plants for problem places and that this is what makes her garden different. The writing itself has an immediacy. She walks through the garden armed with a notebook, seeing all kinds of work that needs to be done. She writes "what I feel then and there," and if that moment is delayed she finds it difficult to work backwards.

Although the garden is alive with visitors, Chatto still sees it as a private place. She delights in talking to visitors, happy to share her experiences and theirs, and welcoming feedback on the planting. While she takes obvious pleasure in appealing so widely through her ideas, she remains modest and honest, which is perhaps the key to her success.

Piet Oudolf

"Structure is the most important component in a successful planting; colour is important too but it is a secondary consideration."

Piet Oudolf

Piet Oudolf (b.1936) looked at landscape gardening as a career alternative to his family business of catering. His great interest was plants, and an early influence was his compatriot Mien Ruys, whose nursery gardens at Dedemsvaart were a source of inspiration for many designers.

The English garden was another point of reference, and Oudolf visited Hidcote Manor in the late 1970s, to experience the planted atmosphere. He and his wife, Anja, also visited Beth Chatto's garden and nursery, returning home impressed by the integration of the two ventures

and determined to work along similar lines. They set up a nursery in Hummelo, near Arnhem, and he collected a range of herbaceous perennials and grasses from across Europe, inspired by Karl Foerster, a major influence on what has become known as the New Perennial Movement.

Oudolf pays great attention to the range of plants he uses, selecting, on the basis of field trials, forms that lend a particular strength to his associations, such as a more luxuriant depth of colour or a prolonged flowering period. As a result his planting design is instantly recognizable, a combination of vibrant hues and structural grasses, often best seen in the golden glow of evening.

His approach has transformed the teaching of planting design across Europe, reinforced by books such as *Designing with Plants, Dream Plants for the*

Left The centrepiece of Oudolf's garden at Hummelo illustrates the main elements of his work – clouds of grasses, tall architectural perennials, and clipped hedges. Spikes, plates, and globes are also frequently used, seen through veils of grass seed heads.

Above Intense flower colour typifies Oudolf's planting. Here, echinacea provides the focus of colour and form, around which other tones and textures are organized. The dynamic border arrangement allows larger plant masses to dominate the foreground for increased drama.

Opposite Oudolf softens the old farm courtyard at Bury Court with mixed, grass-rich perennial planting. Tall spikes of *Stipa gigantea* diffuse the mounded planting associations, while honey-coloured stone setts add to the composition's texture.

Natural Garden, and *Gardening with Grasses*. He also represents the move away from mixed planting and shrub dependence into perennials, which has long been criticized as labour-intensive and demanding. Oudolf has managed to emphasize the dynamic qualities of perennials and, by using plants that are mutually supportive, he also promotes the ease of care.

He selects plants for their vigour, structure, and ability to work well through the winter, when traditionally perennials were cut down and lost in visual terms. His books often show magical images of frosted seed heads and grasses, as if to counter the claims that shrubs and evergreens are the only options. To some extent, this effect, seen less often in Britain's milder climate, relies on the hot summers and cold winters that are typical of the Netherlands and Germany.

Many of Oudolf's most prestigious schemes have been in England, including two herbaceous borders at the Royal Horticultural Society's headquarters at Wisley, Surrey. Waves of colour and texture run across these like huge ripples, and liners have been buried underground to maintain a distinct separation between the blocks of plants.

Oudolf often uses precise topiary among his softer associations. His own garden at Hummelo shows this method well, with horizontal runs of wave-trimmed hedges acting as a foil to light-catching grasses, deep purple-red astrantia, and the almost monstrous *Angelica gigas*. In the nursery, silver-leafed pear (*Pyrus salicifolia*) provides tall, structural columns to punctuate the beds.

In partnership with Arne Maynard, Oudolf created the garden that won the coveted Best in Show award at the 2000 Chelsea Flower Show in London. This was a structured design that incorporated the rich and evocative colours so resonant of his work, with salvia, *Centranthus*, and *Cimicifuga* combined to form a rich purple-red tapestry. Spires of *Cirsium rivulare* 'Atropurpureum' complemented to perfection the rich-red reredos used behind a wall of water, the focus of the garden.

Elsewhere Oudolf has enjoyed great success with his extensive design and planting. Good examples are the Dromparken, at Enköping, Sweden, and the gardens of the Pensthorpe Waterfowl Trust in Norfolk. One of his most interesting ventures is the garden at Bury Court, Hampshire, a space attached to a private house and working nursery, and therefore close to his heart.

Some of Oudolf's ground plans lack the subtlety of his planting, owing to his enthusiasm for asymmetry and unusual geometry. But the vibrancy of the planting, always given prominence in deep and generous beds, more than makes up for these idiosyncrasies.

More than any other designer, Oudolf has promoted the use of grasses in the garden border. Their ability to soften and fill out borders with billowing, shimmering seed heads has transformed the look of gardens around the world. In addition their ease of maintenance and prolonged season of interest have been acknowledged and welcomed by amateurs and professionals alike.

Oudolf hopes also to conquer the public realm of planting design, bringing herbaceous perennials and grasses back into our public spaces. Given the zeal with which he addressed the transformation of the garden border in the late twentieth century, there can be little doubt that we shall be enjoying enriched public spaces in the near future.

Dan Pearson

"We should not feel separate from nature, we are part of it. We need to cover our footprints."

Dan Pearson

Dan Pearson (b.1964) has clear memories of his earliest encounters with a garden. When he was a child, his family moved into a house and garden that both needed complete refurbishment, and he well remembers being involved with clearance and the thrill at discovering original planting, lost for years under a sea of undergrowth.

As a teenager, Pearson worked as a gardener at Greatham Mill, Hampshire. The owner, Mrs Pumphrey, taught him a great deal about planting and how to work with colour. Study at Wisley and Kew fed his interest in plants, and by this time he had received his first commission, to design a

garden for Frances Mossman. She was later the owner of Home Farm, Northamptonshire, one of his most famous projects.

While he was at college, Pearson visited northern Spain and the "Valley of the Flowers" in the Himalayas, as well as spending a year with arid and desert planting in Jerusalem. This led him to understand that "nature was far superior in her plant associations than man could ever be."

Beth Chatto also remains a major influence. She seems to Pearson to understand nature and its teaching, associating plants in a much more ecological way than her predecessors. Thomas Church is another hero, revealing a cleanliness in his design structure and a real sense of place. Pearson feels that Church's work shares a timelessness with the architectural spaces of Luis Barragán and the sensuous forms of Isamu Noguchi.

Left The gardens of Home Farm provided Pearson with the perfect canvas for his planting design work. The diffusing veils of *Stipa gigantea*, interplanted with spikes of eremurus and the smaller heads of knautia, produce a light, diaphanous effect.

Pearson's approach to garden design is still evolving, and the degree of emphasis that he places on planting is changing dramatically. Although he is above all a horticulturist, it is the spatial quality that he currently finds most satisfying. He would like to feel that he has worked with subtlety and that the message of his designs would be "quiet but profound, seen as part of a place and grounded when you are within them."

Pearson looks for his own gut reaction to the sites on which he works, a feeling that must be recognized as part of the design process. The first ten minutes of any visit put him in touch with the site or landscape, and later in the project he spends time observing the different qualities of light or the impact of the seasons. Most of his projects are long-term ones, and he welcomes the chance to share the development of his design ideas with clients.

He is currently making a garden in the South Downs, the rolling chalk landscape of southern England. He has set out to blur the boundaries between garden and landscape, seeing the design as land art, sculpting the ground, and paring back the planting to maximize this expression. The planting palette throughout is muted and spare, in line with Pearson's new philosophy.

An early interest in landscape design is now being satisfied through his work, although he regrets none of his adventures in the exploration of planting since the early 1980s. One of his recent trips was to the Bloedel Reserve, on Bainbridge Island, off Seattle, Washington. Here he explored the work of Thomas Church, "a moss garden in a savage environment and very much in tune with my approach."

Pearson is happy to continue on his path of evolutionary change, and acknowledges that his planting is undergoing a transformation. Whereas today he would use five species, only a year ago he would have selected ten for the same scheme. He finds also that a wider concern for the environment is increasingly governing his work. As a result, while his footprint as a designer seems to be lighter, it is no less powerful in character.

Above In a garden produced for television Pearson uses gently contoured retaining walls to reinforce the lines of the planting drifts and to lead the eye into the space. The interplay of hard and soft materials gives the garden its character.

Right Home Farm's gardens are divided into a number of spaces, each with its own character. These spaces are designed to flow together through the use of planting as the defining spatial element.

William Robinson

The English Flower Garden, the best-known book by William Robinson (1838–1935), was first published in 1883; it ran to fifteen editions in his lifetime and adorned the shelves of avid gardeners far from the shores of England. Although most of his life preceded the twentieth century, the impact of this gardener and writer lives on to the present day, influencing the concepts of New Perennial planting now prevalent in western Europe.

Although Robinson's gardens are few, his prolific writing exerted a great influence. This is seen most strikingly in his feud with Reginald Blomfield, who argued against him in favour of a more formal, architectural quality to the garden. Blomfield produced more gardens and landscapes than Robinson but lost this stylistic battle.

Below While Robinson allowed a certain formality to creep into his ground plans, the planting was soft and informal. At Gravetye Manor, simple planting combinations of wisteria, iris, and nepeta soften the paving layout, letting the plants dominate.

In *The Wild Garden*, first published in 1870, Robinson argued for the use of hardy exotic plants under conditions where they would thrive without further care. A look at the work of most modern designers and plantsmen shows that this concept still holds true.

Robinson railed against formal design, yet this is in evidence at Gravetye Manor, his home in East Sussex. He campaigned against bedding, yet Vita Sackville-West noticed his use of pansies under his roses. Many have suggested that he was somewhat arrogant, criticizing almost everything that others did but never finding fault with his own work. This opinionated approach has proved popular. Through journals such as *The Garden* (now part of *Homes and Gardens*) and *Gardening Illustrated* he reached a mass audience and perhaps became the first garden-maker to understand the power of published work.

Beatrix Farrand, Gertrude Jekyll, and Vita Sackville-West, to name but three fellow gardeners, worshipped Robinson, learning and disseminating his teaching on naturalistic and informal planting. Jekyll wrote the section on colour for *The English Flower Garden*, but she may have contributed much more. Even so, her association with Robinson did not stop her using clipped yew hedges for structure, a concept frequently derided in his writing.

Robinson was born in Ireland, working at first as a gardener before going to study at the National Botanic Garden in Glasnevin. An important development in his outlook came after he moved to England in 1861 and worked at the Royal Botanic Garden in Regent's Park, London. It was this experience that fired his interest in wild or native plants. An ambitious young man, he also moved into journalism.

Gravetye Manor, which Robinson purchased with the proceeds from his writing, is his main garden work. Here he was able to plant drifts of daffodils, develop his woodland garden, and enjoy his meadow communities. He idealized the simplicity of cottage gardens and their old-fashioned plants, using this as a basis for his philosophy and thus influencing garden-making throughout the world for over a hundred years.

Beatrix Farrand

In the privileged world of wealthy America in the late nineteenth and early twentieth centuries it would have been easy to sit back and enjoy life. Beatrix Farrand (1872–1959) was part of that society but yearned for something more. Her great interest was the garden and the wider landscape.

As the niece of the novelist Edith Wharton, Farrand undoubtedly used her social connections to develop her skills as a gardener, but she also read widely and was influenced by William Robinson, whom she met and corresponded with regularly, and by Gertrude Jekyll. Farrand studied technical drawing, learning as much as possible from other professionals and working at one time with Frederick Law Olmsted. Landscape architecture would not have been taught at university, and, as a woman, Farrand would not have had access to academic courses. It is a tribute to her endurance and passion for landscape design that she became the only woman founder of the American Society of Landscape Architects (ASLA).

Farrand's most famous work is Dumbarton Oaks, in Washington DC, originally created for Mildred and Robert Woods Bliss but now bequeathed to Harvard University. On the face of it this is an Italianate garden with planting influenced by Jekyll, but Farrand created an American solution that makes the garden belong to its location. This ability to apply her critical awareness was sufficient to ensure a departure from cliché and pastiche in this and many other gardens and landscapes.

By the end of her career she had produced over 200 commissions, mainly in the United States but also in England, working with Leonard and Dorothy Elmhirst at Dartington Hall in Devon.

Perhaps Farrand's greatest achievement was to save Gertrude Jekyll's drawings from destruction in the Second World War. Her own collected works, along with the Jekyll drawings, were left to the University of California. These papers came to light when Betty Massingham was researching Jekyll – a study that led to a revival of interest in the 1970s, the effects of which are still felt today.

Above Dumbarton Oaks is Farrand's most famous work. Designed in a formal manner, but overlaid with rich and informal planting groups, it was influenced by William Robinson and Gertrude Jekyll. In a sequence of descending terraces, the soft planting and hard structure combine to turn the garden to the landscape that lies beyond.

Jens Jensen

Born in Denmark, Jens Jensen (1860–1951) emigrated to the United States in 1884, eventually settling in Chicago. At first he worked as a gardener but he subsequently became a landscape architect, practising mainly in the public realm. By 1920 he had decided to concentrate much more on private commissions.

Jensen became fascinated by the indigenous plants of his adopted country, and his work later became synonymous with the "Prairie Style." His wild, expansive approach suited public spaces well, yet he became the favoured landscape designer of the architect Frank Lloyd Wright, collaborating on a range of private houses and gardens, such as the Coonley and Booth residences, both ground-breaking houses built in the early twentieth century.

Although he was not a native American, or perhaps because of this, Jensen felt the huge and resonant impact of the prairie landscape. He lived in Chicago in the late nineteenth century, when the prairie would have been evident all around the city. He was struck by the surrounding sea of grass, and as a result is one of the earliest protagonists of naturalistic garden design, creating a line of descent that includes the partnership of Wolfgang Oehme and James van Sweden.

Although Jensen's work was covered in American design journals, he remained a rather solitary figure in his profession. One of his largest undertakings was the Lincoln Memorial Garden, in Springfield, Illinois, begun in 1933. The scheme covers 24ha (59 acres) and consists of a sequence of meadows, each one given over to a single species or association. Some seventy years after its creation, it is difficult to differentiate between art and nature.

Jensen's professional relationship with Wright broke down as the architect was more interested in sculpted or man-made form, while Jensen was wrapped up in nature and the creation of habitats. He committed many of his thoughts to his book, *Siftings*, published in 1939, and is remembered mainly in academic circles – indeed, it can be said that Jensen failed to achieve mainstream popularity. His school, The Clearing, in Wisconsin, survives as a testament to his pioneering work and his ambition to increase environmental awareness.

Rosemary Weisse

Towards the end of the twentieth century a new approach to planting design came to fruition. In reality this was a seamless evolution that linked William Robinson and Gertrude Jekyll with Karl Foerster and George Arends, leading eventually to long-term experimentation with herbaceous perennials at the University of Weihenstephan in Germany. Professor Richard Hansen carried out much of this research, published with Friedrich Stahl in *Perennials and their Garden Habitats*.

What all of these individuals shared was an interest in the development of successful planting habitats, and, more recently, a sense of sustainability. This idea is particularly applied to perennials, which were often shunned as maintenance became, in the second half of the century, a serious issue for both public and private gardens.

The German landscape architect Rosemary Weisse pulled together many of these threads in her planting for Munich's Westpark, part of the 1983 International Garden Festival. The development of the site was shared with other designers, but it is Weisse's work here that has become an icon of twentieth-century planting design.

The approach is often called the "steppe" style, generally using low perennials and grasses to form a continuous cover of plants. Larger or more imposing perennials are used for emphasis, while shrubs or trees are employed for more permanent or screening structure. In contrast to the traditional herbaceous border, maintenance is minimal, and the ground is covered by a gravel mulch. The plants are not fed, and the fertility of the soil is purposely kept low. Although the planting cannot escape attack by weeds, the dense carpet of planting reduces this problem, and the offending plants are removed before they can set seed. Plants are often small as a result of low soil fertility, but they are resilient, and the selection of good companions reduces or eradicates over-vigorous spreading and self-seeding. It is these problems that call for long-term maintenance in the traditional border.

Weisse has handled the planting well and extended the season of interest, to the delight of the local community and regular users of the park.

She sees herself as painting a picture that nature eventually takes over. The planting is a place of pilgrimage for garden and landscape designers, and its influence is noticeable in the work of Christopher Bradley-Hole, Piet Oudolf, Wolfgang Oehme and James van Sweden, and Dan Pearson.

Following Weisse's example, the adoption of a matrix or grid into which a complex and random planting pattern is introduced has become increasingly common. In addition, the widespread acceptance of ornamental grasses as an integral part of modern planting design has stemmed to a great extent from Weisse's work and that of her European contemporaries, such as Urs Walser in Dresden, and Heine Lutz in Stuttgart.

Below Weisse's loose and meadow-like "steppe" planting for the Westpark, in Munich, has close links with Jens Jensen's work and epitomizes the New Perennial approach to planting that dominated garden design in the late twentieth century. Here, grasses and non-vigorous perennials such as *Centranthus ruber* and phlox are used against cotinus, which has a structural role in the design.

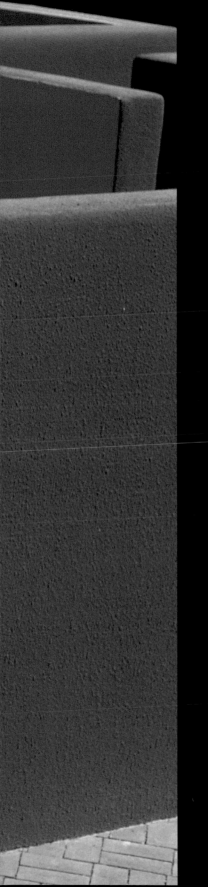

CONCEPT

A s the profession of landscape and garden design flourished during the twentieth century, so the intellectual and academic processes of teaching and learning came to be woven into the designer's work. Design development began to involve a much deeper analysis of site, context, and specific location, as well as of the personality, personal history, and aspirations of the client than previously. The identification of a design concept or overriding theme began to play an increasingly important role in the development of successful and imaginative design solutions.

Architects such as Le Corbusier (in his early work), Frank Lloyd Wright, and Richard Neutra were responsible for associating their built forms directly with the surrounding landscape, often allowing it to flow through the site and around the building. The sense of place took on a new meaning, which required landscape and garden designers to develop an awareness of where they were working. Thomas Church illustrates this with his sublime El Novillero garden in the Sonoma Valley, California, in which he allows the distant meandering river that flows lazily to the sea to infiltrate his structured design with sensuous and fluid curves.

This intellectual response is most often linked with the later work of Geoffrey Jellicoe, who became interested in the subconscious and man's relationship to his wider environment, as well as in contemporary art and the concept of abstraction. In an essay in *Denatured Visions: Landscape and Culture in the Twentieth Century*, edited by Stuart Wrede and William Howard Adams, he wrote: "Jung states clearly that the subconscious (feeling or instinct) lives a life of its own, independent of the conscious (the intellect); that each, operating separately, can be ineffectual and even chaotic; that opposition of one to another can be catastrophic; but that in unison they can create the great works of civilisation." Jung referred in his own writing to the "loss of soul," a concept that Jellicoe strove to consider in most of his later commissions. He aimed to reconcile the landscapes he created with the client and to blend human and natural elements. Later, he revelled in the influence of modern art, being excited by his contemporaries and their obvious passion and inspiration.

This link with modern, often conceptual, art marked a specific change in the direction of landscape and garden design. The influence of the thinking, the process, and the end product that was a synthesis of these became absorbed into the design process. Art and landscape had been linked before, with the Picturesque Movement of the eighteenth century, and William Kent in particular. However, this was design that reproduced a view or sequence of views, using the imagery of painters such as Lorrain and Poussin, rather than adopting

Above To create the path that leads to the Kennedy Memorial, at Runnymede, just outside London, Geoffrey Jellicoe used a series of granite setts, every one different. These are intended to evoke a sense of pilgrimage in visitors as they ascend the gentle hill from the River Thames to the simple stone monument.

Previous pages Martha Schwartz produces conceptual installations for public and private spaces around the world. In the garden of the Davis residence, El Paso, Texas, she uses adobe walls washed in deep colours to create a variety of spatial experiences.

The idea of a design concept, or overriding theme, was not always recognized as playing a major role in the evolution of successful garden design. Arts and Crafts gardens were usually plant-led compositions, compartmentalized to allow a wide variety of diverse species to be displayed and organized. They were often introverted designs and invited a sequential progress through the various spaces, frequently divorced from and uninterested in their actual location and sense of place. Edwin Lutyens was one of the few architects who managed to relate his gardens to their context, partly through carefully controlled views, but also through his choice of construction materials.

It was only with the advent of modernism and the loss of axial dominance that gardens began to relate more directly to their landscape. There are links to the English Landscape School, although these landscape gardens were heavily manipulated.

the artistic process itself. Allegory was used, but often this was related to prose or poetry, rather than relying on purely visual communication. Here, for the first time, art was absorbed into the garden, and the boundary between art and design began to blur.

If Jellicoe was fascinated by abstraction and saw the work of modern artists such as Ben Nicholson or Henry Moore as a resource for his creativity, Isamu Noguchi fused design and art in a single approach to spatial manipulation. His philosophy was entirely sculptural; he thought of sculpture as harmonizing and humanizing spaces. He was also able to fuse the philosophies of East and West, expanding his creativity from sculpture to furniture, lighting, landscape, and playgrounds. The resulting gardens and landscapes were indeed sculptural and esoteric, although function often

also played an essential part. Given the breadth of Noguchi's endeavours in furniture, lighting, interior, and garden design, it was not surprising that this artistic bias was evident.

Garrett Eckbo was heavily influenced by other modernists such as Christopher Tunnard and Thomas Church. The quality of spatial control enthused him most, and the way in which Japanese gardens and landscapes achieved a balance between solid and void was particularly inspiring, a quality that impacted on the whole world of design in the early twentieth century. Eckbo was fascinated and excited by the development in the architecture school at Harvard, particularly after the introduction of Walter Gropius in 1937, who had been brought to the United States from England. The modern approach that Gropius represented eventually infected the landscape

Below Isabelle Greene is inspired by the landscape of her native California. In this garden on the Gulf of Carpinteria, she uses the ocean as a theme, with the gently curving decks producing wave-like ripples. Planting is carefully positioned to give maximum light and uninterrupted views.

school, particularly Eckbo, Dan Kiley, and James Rose, transforming design and design teaching for the rest of the twentieth century. In William Howard Adams's *Grounds for Change: Major Gardens of the Twentieth Century*, Eckbo is quoted thus: "Basically it made it possible to eliminate preconceived design vocabularies, and to develop forms and arrangements which spoke to specific sites, clients, local contexts and regional cultures."

In 1983 Ed Bye published his classic book *Art into Landscape, Landscape into Art*, in which he discussed the creative concepts and intellectual development of design in terms of the designer's response to the landscape. Concept became a controlling factor that directed and supported the design process and thinking. Bye refined the understanding of site and location with designs that emphasized the subtlety of their place – the intervention of the designer becoming so delicate as to be almost invisible.

Isabelle Greene also works in this way, finding inspiration in the landscape, particularly of her native California. Land form, vegetation, rock strata, and wilderness all contribute to her design solutions, which are sensitive and appropriate to their location. Greene also spends a great deal of time talking with her clients at the important briefing stage, familiarizing herself with their personalities and experiences.

In the second half of the twentieth century conceptual design, art, and science moved closer together, and the boundary between the three – if that ever really mattered – became indistinct. Design started to move away from accepted or traditional pedagogics, and much more experimental and emotive work developed in the universities and spread out into the field. Many of these practitioners returned to teach this new "art in the landscape."

In the United States, Peter Walker and Martha Schwartz represent a school of conceptually based design thinking that produced design solutions that echoed a sense of place, abstracted the essence of a client or a location, and delivered messages

Below The Bagel Garden, in Boston, Massachusetts, put its creator, Martha Schwartz, firmly on the design stage. The garden was partly intended as a witty gift to a friend returning home, but it was also a challenge to the accepted thinking about landscape and garden design.

that were variously subtle, humorous, or profound. Schwartz's turf mounds for the Minneapolis Federal Courthouse Plaza relate back to the landscape seen by the first settlers – a deep link to experience and location that many might not consider but perhaps subliminally enjoy. Tyre-like objects sit at the base of palm trees at The Citadel, in Commerce, California – a reminder that the building was a tyre factory. The concept was that of an oasis, and remnants of tyres provide seating and protect the trees from parking cars.

Walker's minimal designs continue this thread, producing simple but profound geometric statements in the landscape – installations that cause one to reflect and to attach memory, familiarity, and belonging to new landscapes. Schwartz and Walker originally worked together but have since gone their separate ways, producing startling garden and landscape imagery with a mixture of intellectual endeavour and intuitive response.

Both designers were heavily influenced by the twentieth-century phenomenon of land art, with which their work has much in common. Robert Smithson's *Spiral Jetty* has been particularly influential, as have installations by artists Richard Serra, Richard Long, and Michael Heizer. The monumental scale on which these men work is evident in the commissions of both Walker and Schwartz, as is the communication of a deep-seated message. The land art that flourished in the twentieth century represents a return to the mounds and monuments created in prehistory.

The work of Charles Jencks uses the development of the universe and its links with our cultural development as a basis for an allegorical garden that is very much of the late twentieth century but is also linked to the landscape gardens of William Kent. There is a progress and a sequence related to the experience of the garden. At one time the champion and theorizer of post-modernism, Jencks has journeyed through an intellectual approach to architecture and into chaos theory. For him, the garden is imposed on the landscape rather than growing from it, in a return to the pre-modern idiom in which concept is related to philosophical thought rather than to a

specific sense of place or memory. Again, the landscape can be enjoyed on many levels, but it is a place to be savoured and considered.

There is room for all of these conceptual and subconscious strands, and indeed both landscape design and garden design have been enriched and diversified by their growing relationship with artistic expression and communication. The gradual coalescence of artistic and design endeavours has produced some of the most memorable works of the twentieth century.

Above Peter Walker uses form and geometry to express his ideas, often creating graphic and powerful imagery in the process. In his garden for the Centre for Advanced Science and Technology, in the new town of Harima, Japan, carefully positioned stepping stones and raked gravel are resonant of the Japanese tradition.

Geoffrey Jellicoe

"…our consciousness does not create itself – it wells up from unknown depths. In childhood it awakens gradually and all through life it wakes each morning out of the depths of sleep."

Carl Gustav Jung

Geoffrey Jellicoe (1900–96) spanned the twentieth century in his life and his work. Involved with the inauguration and development of Britain's Landscape Institute and the promotion of landscape design as a respected profession, he later became president of the Institute, before taking up the presidency of the International Federation of Landscape Architects.

Writing was Jellicoe's first interest, a skill to which he returned on numerous occasions, producing important texts such as *The Landscape of Man*, *The Oxford Companion to Gardens*, and, his first

Left Jellicoe's incorporation of a sculptural wall by Ben Nicholson at Sutton Place, Surrey, represents the achievement of his long-held ambition to site modern art in the landscape. The huge marble relief is set among water and dark foliage to maximize the sense of atmosphere.

book, *Italian Gardens of the Renaissance* (1925). The latter, co-authored with J.C. Shepherd, resulted from Jellicoe's time in Rome studying architecture. He and Shepherd toured Italy together, photographing and drawing gardens, and the two designers were later to collaborate successfully.

Jellicoe's first break came in the early 1930s: a café and garden at Cheddar Gorge, Somerset, on which he worked with Russell Page. Ditchley Park, Oxfordshire, followed – a commission for Ronald Tree, who, fifty years later, invited Jellicoe to design the gardens at Shute House, Dorset. Page also brought in influential clients, including the then Duke and Duchess of York, who required a garden for Royal Lodge in Windsor Great Park, Berkshire.

Through his teaching, Jellicoe was introduced to the work of Le Corbusier, but it is interesting

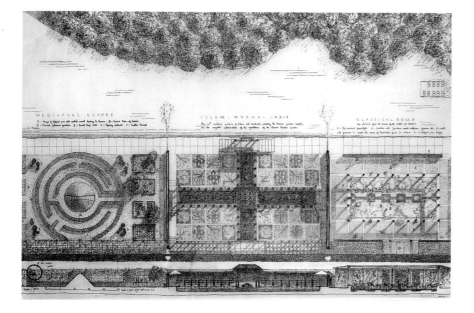

Above The task of creating botanic gardens in Galveston, Texas, for the Moody Foundation, enabled Jellicoe to indulge his favourite passions of garden history and conceptual development. The gardens, seen here as design drawings, used historical design evolution as the means of associating and interpreting plant material.

Opposite The musical cascade at Shute House, Dorset, provides the centrepiece to the garden, a shining rill of water dropping through textured planting and contoured lawns. Jellicoe's two principal gardens, Shute House and Sutton Place, both achieve their impact through a combination of geometry and the art of the subconscious.

that this was a vicarious pleasure. Jellicoe seems to stand apart from the developments in design that should have excited him, although he did try to engage Christopher Tunnard as a tutor at the AA before the Second World War, realizing that Tunnard's approach was full of promise. Jellicoe was hardly old at the time, but his outlook may be explained by the conservativism of his clientele.

His interest in the modern world was fired much later by the garden designer Frederick Gibberd. They were great friends, and Jellicoe became fascinated by Gibberd's collection of modern art. When Gibberd told him that the works inspired him greatly as a designer, a door seemed to open for Jellicoe. He later freely used paintings and sculpture as sources for his own work, and eventually became a champion of the Swiss psychoanalyst Carl Gustav Jung. Jellicoe's adoption of the art and philosophy of the collective unconscious in support of his creative work can be seen in the water gardens he designed for Hemel Hempstead, Hertfordshire, and enlivened with hidden meaning. Inspired by the art of Paul Klee, Jellicoe saw in his design the shape of a serpent, which came to dominate the whole commission as a controlling concept.

Jellicoe admired the artist Ben Nicholson, eventually using his work to great effect at Sutton Place, Surrey, for the Texan millionaire Stanley Seeger. He had already produced many prestigious schemes, but it was Sutton Place that projected

him into the public eye, at the age of eighty. A famous garden, it seems, is much more identifiable with its designer than is a famous landscape.

Jellicoe, who saw each garden as an expression of the client, approached Seeger with some trepidation. However, Jellicoe found that Seeger was enthusiastic about his ideas on the subconscious and they agreed to explore the garden conceptually.

Schemes in Modena and Brescia followed, and Jellicoe was later approached by the Moody Foundation to create a botanical garden in Texas. The Galveston Gardens were initially created as part of a grand design that was rejected; the accepted design was later based on an exploration of gardens and plants through history. The client wanted a new form of botanic garden that would attract a wide variety of visitors – almost a planted theme park. The concept was a tableau of designed landscape 1.6km (1 mile) in length – a feat for any designer, let alone an octogenarian.

As he got older, Jellicoe began to do less design work, although he still found the energy to return to writing. In Canada, in 1983 he delivered the Guelph Lectures, his collected thoughts on landscape design, published in 1987 to wide acclaim as *The Guelph Lectures on Landscape Design.*

Jellicoe's most memorable work is that dedicated to President John F. Kennedy, created in England's historic Runnymede meadow, beside the River Thames, near London The client committee specified that the memorial should appeal to visitors on an intellectual level, giving Jellicoe the opportunity to experiment with his Jungian approach. The design is eminently simple but full of symbolism, and is inspired by John Bunyan's *Pilgrim's Progress* of 1678. The route is allegorically paved with 60,000 hand-crafted granite setts, selected to symbolize a host of individuals, as no two setts would be the same. Here, the landscape – rather than the inscribed tablet – is the memorial.

When Jellicoe's work is considered as a whole, what will be remembered is his conceptual design, his inspirational writing, and his intellectual approach to landscape and garden design.

Isamu Noguchi

*"The garden of the Yale library ... is purely that of the imagination;
it is nowhere yet somehow familiar. Its size is fictive, of infinite
space, or cloistered containment."*

Isamu Noguchi

Isamu Noguchi (1904–88) is the twentieth century's bridge between the design philosophies of East and West, placing emphasis on spatial design and the manipulation of forms in space.

At eighteen, the Japanese-born Noguchi was apprenticed to the sculptor Guzon Borgium and, after moving to New York, developed his interest in design through evening classes. Later, he branched out into stage and costume design. The American architect Buckminster Fuller was influential in developing Noguchi's sense of space and his use of technology and new materials. Noguchi also

worked with the legendary dancer Martha Graham, producing many sets. He would explore theatrical qualities of the garden in a similar way, regarding space as a volume to be treated sculpturally.

In the late 1930s Noguchi became fascinated by playgrounds and play equipment, as well as the ground itself, and the way in which it could be sculpted. He created a design for a contoured playground and presented the work to the New York Parks Department. The scheme, like many of Noguchi's landscapes, remains on paper.

Two other unrealized works set him on the road to garden and landscape design. The first was a joint design with Edward Durrell Stone for the Jefferson Memorial Park in St Louis, Missouri. The second later became known as *The Sculpture to Be Seen from Mars*. Noguchi had become concerned

Left Noguchi responded sculpturally to space and place, allowing the balance of mass and void to create visual excitement. *To the Issei* was installed at the Japanese-American Cultural Center Plaza in Los Angeles, an expression of Noguchi's shared roots.

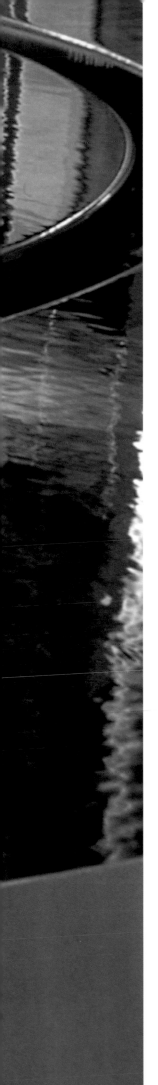

Peter Walker

"More than ever, we need ... spaces for discovery, repose, and privacy in our increasingly bewildering, spiritually impoverished, overstuffed, and undermaintained garden Earth."

Peter Walker

It would be easy to label Peter Walker (b.1932) as a minimalist, but when we use any tag the detail and message is often lost or diluted, and in Walker's case such a description would not do justice to the spiritual significance of his work. His designs display a strong sense of space, so it comes as no surprise to find that the work of André Le Nôtre has been a huge influence.

Walker delights in the contrast of formality with nature, bringing sharply defined shapes into competition with softer vegetation or arranging plants into regimented lines or patterns. Many of

his larger schemes use shapes, forms, and patterns that work well from above, creating parterre designs for the twentieth and twenty-first centuries. The garden for the Hotel Kempinski, in Munich, is a grid-based parterre garden with a secondary, overlapping, angled grid that creates a complex pattern of angles and a sense of rhythm.

At one time Walker worked with Martha Schwartz, and they share a penchant for land art. Walker goes further and sees himself making marks on the landscape that relate to an ancient tradition, the results of which can be seen across the world.

Themes and imagery play a part in linking ideas to their specific locations in Walker's designs. The gardens that make up the Centre for Advanced Science and Technology, Japan, are redolent of ancient Japanese gardens translated to

Left Supremely precise detailing and an eye for minimalist quality mark much of Walker's work. Designed in this spirit is a stainless-steel pool at the Plaza Tower complex, Costa Mesa, California, a fascinating feature that invites a close inspection of its dark interior and shimmering geometry.

In the Toyota Municipal Museum of Art in Japan the lake contains a huge, circular air fountain, producing a ring of white water that disturbs the otherwise calm, reflective surface. Only visible from a distance, the circle appears both mysterious and fascinating.

Perhaps this designer's most serene and technically accomplished design, however, is that for the Plaza Tower and Park, Costa Mesa, California. The whole complex consists of stylized landscapes, but at the base of the main tower is a pool made up of concentric rings of reflecting water, retained by a skin of stainless steel to produce razor-sharp edges. The water shimmers, moving only to slip over the edges into deep rills. The pattern of the water continues through the abstract patterns of paving stones, selected and placed to give varying degrees of light reflection.

Walker includes among his more recent influences Garrett Eckbo, Thomas Church, and Lawrence Halprin. However, it is Dan Kiley – a designer also deeply influenced by Le Nôtre – who is pre-eminent for him. There is certainly a classical quality evident in the work of both Walker and Kiley that seems to sit happily alongside their modernist credentials.

Recently Walker has become fascinated by the gardens of the modern age, researching and discovering the story of modernism in the United States through the production of the book *Invisible Gardens: The Search for Modernism in the American Landscape*. He feels somehow cheated of a full training in design history, and the project allowed him to fill in some of the gaps.

More than anything, Walker's commissions represent a hybridization of philosophies, with influence and inspiration coming from land artists such as Michael Heizer and Robert Smithson, notably the latter's *Spiral Jetty*; artists such as Jasper Johns and Yves Klein; and sculptors such as Andy Goldsworthy and Richard Serra. In his writing, Walker talks of the loss of expression in the process of modern abstraction and the resultant loss of faith. In his own work, he strives to restore expression, spirituality, and a sense of profound contact with the natural world.

Above The centrepiece of Japan's Centre for Advanced Science and Technology is a fusion of Eastern and Western design philosophies. Raked gravel, stepping stones, and conical "mountains" are brought together in a simple open space, emphasizing the sculptural forms and their symbolic power.

Opposite A wider view of the shimmering water feature for Plaza Tower by Peter Walker and Partners shows the precision detailing for which the practice is famous. The sophisticated combination of water paving and planting creates a sense of ripling movement.

the twentieth century. Walker uses stone, moss, and grass to create "mountains" – cones that are monumental and provide a link with the gardens of the Muromachi period (1338–1573) in Japan.

The gardens include raked gravel setts with highly polished "piers" of granite, mist fountains to swirl around tall bamboos, and huge burnt logs to provide counterpoint. The use of the various gardens for quiet contemplation and the careful placement of stepping stones are also both Japanese in origin, and lend the whole complex an air of sophisticated thoughtfulness and calm.

Walker engages in the production of large public landscapes. Their scale allows dramatic concepts to emerge, often combined with clever and witty details or installations. The Tanner Fountain, Massachusetts, is a perefect circle of stones from which emerges a fine mist that sits over the rugged boulders like a ghostly shroud.

Martha Schwartz

"I like to see and understand a space, to hear everyone's point of view in order to respond to many different needs."

Martha Schwartz

Martha Schwartz (b.1950) began her career in fine art, studying printmaking in Michigan, but found herself fascinated by land art. The work of practitioners such as Robert Smithson, Nancy Holt, and Michael Heizer jumped from the confines of the studio and into the landscape on a large scale. Schwartz was keen to apply her artistic training in this way.

At that time landscape architecture was skill-based and regarded as technical rather than artistic. A generally conservative alliance of practitioners appeared to be oblivious to the potential for the expansion of their work and, in a characteristically humorous aside, Schwartz suggested that her individualistic approach "was like farting in church."

Much of her work may be described as installation, concepts combining artistic expression with functional reality. Her most famous work is the Bagel Garden, in Boston, Massachusetts, created as a joky home-coming present for a friend. Containing a hint of the surreal, it sent ripples through the landscape-architectural establishment. She had the garden photographed, using the powerful images and the opportunity to write about her work and make her mark.

Schwartz takes time to understand the space that is to be transformed. The factors that have brought the space to its current status are all considered, and she sees herself dealing with a specific point in time in a site's history. She brainstorms with her design staff, allowing a range

Left The Dickenson garden, in Santa Fe, is one of Schwartz's most celebrated designs, combining Moorish influences and a contemporary treatment. Cooling water and light shade make the garden a welcoming oasis in the dry landscape of New Mexico.

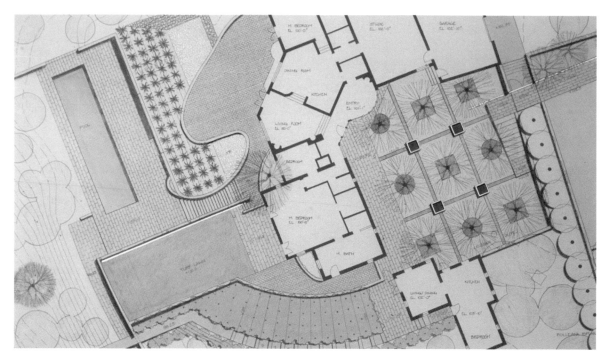

of ideas to be thrown together. She describes the conceptual phase as like dreaming, with the design process and the realization proving greatly thrilling.

She admires the work of Peter Walker for its minimal serenity and that of André Le Nôtre for his outstanding spatial arrangement, which she would be happy indeed to achieve.

In her teaching she tells her students to work intuitively. The designer must consider a huge amount of information, she says, but there is more, and the intuitive must at least be acknowledged.

A strong sense of Schwartz's identity is evident in her work, and, coming from a family background of art and architecture, she sees her artistic sense as its primary engine. She senses that historically Jews were not allowed to follow a profession, and creativity was their response.

Schwartz is very interested in how people use the spaces she designs, how they interact with them, and what they gain from their experience. Some are intimate, such as the Splice Garden, in Cambridge, Massachusetts – a tiny rooftop area that gives the impression of two quite different gardens sharing the same space. The installation was commissioned for a biomedical research centre, the title and concept relating to the genetic engineering carried out there. Other works form huge landscapes, usually urban in character, such as

a new pedestrian square in Manchester, England. The Federal Court Plaza in Minneapolis shares this scale, complete with soft green drumlins and stark paving patterns and textures. All of these designs are alive with vigour and excitement, but each tells another story for those who care enough to reflect on the work in greater depth.

Schwartz strives to make both herself and her clients happy with her concepts and their realization. She admits that her clients must be far-sighted and open-minded enough to travel with her and to enjoy the process too. Her ideas need to remain strong and clear to succeed, and she regards any watering-down of concepts as both unacceptable and unworkable. The results are sometimes dramatic, often humorous, but always imaginative and dynamic. They remain the breath of fresh air that jolted a whole profession into a more artistic and creative mode.

Above The plan of the Dickenson garden reveals a sharp contrast between fluid geometry and regular formality. The main courtyard garden – a grid pattern of brick, gravel, and water – produces a dramatic display of light and colour after dark.

Right In Marina Linear Park, in San Diego, the elegant palm trees are repeated in water through the use of tall steel poles that emit a fine spray. The long avenues of poles produce this light-catching mist on a monumental scale that echoes the expansiveness of the urban space.

FORM

The use of form as an essential element of garden design is a distinctly twentieth-century phenomenon. Three-dimensional form is a part of any spatial design or experience, but its use as an expressive tool has grown out of the Modern Movement and the pure design trajectory that has been followed since the 1920s. In modern garden design, form is celebrated as a sculptural consideration and is often clearly expressed in architectural and planted elements; however, in the flower garden it is frequently lost under a cloud of decoration.

Frank Lloyd Wright

*"All the more because I study Nature do I revere God, because Nature
is all the body of God we will ever know."*

Frank Lloyd Wright

The name of Frank Lloyd Wright (1869–1959) echoes through the twentieth century, usually in relation to architecture and interior design rather than gardens and landscapes. Yet he is a crucial figure in all of these disciplines, an architect who understood the nature of the spaces and locations for which he designed.

He was born in Wisconsin, the son of a Baptist minister who later divorced Wright's mother, Anna; it was she who encouraged her son's architectural leaning. As a child, he was given a set of Froebel building blocks, designed to nurture children's spatial creativity.

Left Fallingwater is Wright's iconic masterpiece, a remarkable synthesis of architecture and landscape, as well as a symbol of the twentieth century's distinctive approach to form and space. The horizontal lines of the cantilevered terraces contrast with the verticals of the forest.

Although Wright at first trained to be a civil engineer, he began his career as a tracer in an architectural practice in Chicago, then a boom town. He moved on to the office of architects Adler and Sullivan, supplementing his income by designing houses in his own time. He was dismissed for breach of contract and immediately started to design the long, low houses that were the trademark of his early career. These "prairie houses" were very much of their place, often linking the prairie-farming tradition with a more contemporary need. They expressed a direct relationship with the natural landscape that surrounded them. In many of his early schemes Wright worked with the garden designer Jens Jensen. Particularly struck by the prairie, Jensen helped to develop a wild exterior to complement the refined lines of the architect's houses.

Christopher Tunnard

"To plant is but a part of landscape composition;
to co-ordinate is all."

Christopher Tunnard

In the period between the two world wars that so dramatically set the twentieth century on a different trajectory, modernism began to dominate the design scene. This new aesthetic rejected what had gone before, favouring change and innovation. Emphasis was placed on function rather than decoration, an approach that many still find difficulty with in relation to gardens.

The Modern Movement began in Europe, emerging from the Bauhaus Design School, established in 1919. The growth of Nazism in the 1930s forced modernists to flee Germany, many travelling to the United States via Britain. As a result, modernism merely brushed the surface of British design, failing to take root. Christopher Tunnard (1910–79) provided the bridge between Europe and America, influencing many designers.

He grew up in Victoria, Canada, before completing his education in architecture and planning in England. Thomas Mawson, a British garden designer and later President of the Institute of Landscape Architects, worked in the United States and Canada and may have advised him.

Tunnard admired the work of Le Corbusier and the French modernists as they looked to the future. After the cataclysm of the First World War, their views must have seemed visionary. Trained in horticulture and construction, he was perfectly positioned to develop the new profession of landscape architecture. He would have known the leaders of the profession, and was approached

Left The wide glass screen of the circular St Ann's Court provides a panoramic view of the undulating garden designed by Christopher Tunnard. From here the eye focuses on the distant cedar glimpsed through a veil of fragrant wisteria that predates the modernist house.

Ted Smyth

"Simplicity, tranquillity, and clarity are the underlying baselines of my best work, and the belief that a garden can be a work of art."

Ted Smyth

In the designs of New Zealander Ted Smyth, (b.1937) the sense of the garden as a work of art comes in part from his background as an artist. After starting his career as a painter and graphic designer, Smyth became interested in both the garden and in landscape. At first, he created gardens as a way of supplementing his income, thereby reactivating the fascination with gardens that he had felt as a child. Eventually he was to devote all of his time to garden design. He is completely self-taught in this discipline, and his conversion to it has affected his whole outlook. "Landscape has become both my life and a way of life," he says.

Left At Quay Park, Smyth experimented with public landscape. The design borrows sacred imagery of New Zealand's Ngati Whatua Iwi tribe, whose permission was needed before this could be used. Their three-fingered hand motif is represented in the elegant water channels.

Smyth has avoided taking reference from the work of other designers, believing that artists must develop a personal vocabulary. Some see this approach as isolationist, but it has produced a freshness and energy that belongs both to Smyth and to his native country. His "vocabulary" has emerged from the earlier interaction between painting and garden design, and also through his deepening interest in materials.

Smyth now feels that he can analyze other approaches from a position of self-confidence. He finds the work of Isamu Noguchi inspiring, spartan, and sculptural, simplified down to a basic essence, and successful as a result. His other major influence is Luis Barragán, whose work is architectural and spatial in concept, manipulating light and shade above all else. Smyth's gardens certainly echo those of these inspirational designers, but, perhaps more important, he derives inspiration from the careful analysis and understanding of particular locations. "My work reflects my attempt to express a sense of place – *Te Papa* – within the wider New Zealand landscape."

He considers Barragán's Fuente del Bebedero and Fuente de Los Amantes (*see p.111*) to be expressions of absolute beauty and power, as a result of their simplicity and spirit. These qualities are likewise present in the four commissions that Smyth feels best exemplify his work.

The Flavell garden was completed in the 1980s and achieves a simple and clear quality. It is a coastal garden, a favourite location of this designer in that it provides a chance to link land and sea with an expansive sense of space. Smyth feels that he was led intuitively through the development of the solution – an approach that often eludes those with an academic training.

Dating from the 1990s, the Sanders garden has a much more contemporary feel. The spaces are architecturally structured around a light and airy glazed pavilion, designed by Rolly Adams. By day, the geometry is bold, while at night subtle and evocative lighting creates a softer garden.

Quay Park is a public space near the docks in Auckland, set on land reclaimed from the sea. The location was once the fishing grounds of the Ngati Whatua Iwi tribe. Smyth uses tribal imagery and symbolism throughout the design, creating crisp and dynamic details with a deeper spiritual message for those willing to explore. He sees this as a poetic journey, providing a significant depth to his work, and feels that the direction he has taken is a natural artistic progression. The attention to detail is remarkable, with lights and directional signs all designed by Smyth to provide consistency. The focus is an elegant, technically accomplished pool and fountain, designed to contrast sacred Maori emblems with contemporary materials.

One of his most recent commissions is on Waiheke Island, in the Hauraki Gulf, where modern architecture and technology blend with a majestic coastal landscape, and there are views of Auckland's skyline. A stunning infinity-edge lap pool catches the city on its axis, and Smyth picks

up the theme of water on both sides of the house, using technology, concrete, and water as a bold but simple statement in a dramatic setting.

Elsewhere on Waiheke, his work includes a scheme for a garden and farm that involves the restoration of native forest. "In this work I feel I have achieved a landscape so subtle and in harmony with its environment that it is not seen as a landscape."

Smyth is proud of the fact that he has, in the past, worked alone, developing design concept and detail single-handedly, and exploring each project in depth. More recently, however, he has collaborated with Rod Barnett on public and civic schemes on a larger scale.

His planting is architectural in quality, to compete with the sleek construction and abstract geometry. The palette is unashamedly native, using sharp, sword-like leaves and textured foliage. As a result, the gardens of this once-remote archipelago have taken centre stage at the beginning of the tweny-first century, having shaken off the slavish copying of European icons in favour of a new and innovative approach that is better suited to its natural beauty. Smyth is seen as a leading figure in this movement and now exerts his own influence as a sought-after and successful designer.

Above A stunning infinity-edge pool on Waiheke Island relates the glass-and-concrete house to the Hauraki Gulf and the distant view of Auckland. Smyth contrasts the rolling slopes of the countryside with sharp concrete walls, pools, and terraces in this uncompromising and refreshing landscape design.

Kathryn Gustafson

*"Designing a landscape is about connecting the body, soul and mind
to the land and to itself."*

Kathryn Gustafson

In certain people's work, landscape design and landscape art merge. Kathryn Gustafson (b.1951) is one such designer who likes to work on a heroic scale, sculpting and massaging the land into evocative and often sensuous forms.

Born in Washington DC, she studied fashion in New York and became fascinated by the qualities of textiles, their movement and fluidity, and the way in which they disguised and covered the form beneath. Her work took her to France, which she was later to make her home.

The link with landscape design came with a yearning for the larger scale. After seeing the work

of the contemporary French designer Jacques Sqard, she went to study in Versailles, and her new career began in earnest in 1980. Since then she has made her mark with a series of substantial conceptually based commissions and now enjoys a reputation for drama matched with sensitivity.

Isamu Noguchi is an influential figure for Gustafson, and his sculptural approach is a match for her own thinking. Kandinsky also inspires her, and the liveliness of his composition contains the contrasts of angle and curve, hard and soft, that resonate through her work. In its relationship to art her work has a spiritual essence that demands closer inspection. The work of Richard Tuttle and Peter Rice has also had an impact on her design thinking.

Gustafson's most famous work is the landscape for Shell Petroleum's headquarters in Rueil-Malmaison, near Paris. The concept for the

proposal revolved around the extraction of fossil fuels and the sense of layers in the earth's crust; fossil remains, and the sense of emergent elements. The most memorable aspect is the entry garden – a sequence of walls emerging from contoured lawns, draped like fabric over reclining forms.

In a more ambitious venture, Gustafson won a competition to design a new park for the town of Terrasson-la-Villedieu, where she lives. The brief called for a composition inspired by historically important gardens from various parts of the world. The result was a design based on the elements common in gardens through history, rather than direct copies or reconstructions. A deconstructed landscape emerged, a sequence of ideas literally tied together with ribbon (*see p.91*). The ribbon itself, in gilded aluminium, is the directional signpost that runs through the entire site, hanging mysteriously from tree canopies.

The preferred scale for Gustafson is echoed in her stunning design for the Rights of Man Square in Évry, near Paris. The square was required to cope with the expansion of the town, and the brief asked for a consideration of the Rights of Man, as embodied in the French constitution.

Freedom of expression is a fundamental element of the Rights of Man, and Gustafson selected this as the basis of the design concept. The square was created to provide spaces for public speaking and debate, theatre, and performance, and to offer its users an inviting and lively experience.

The whole square was lowered to create a protective environment, and the design is based on a tight geometric grid. Part of the square is devoted to dancing jets of water that emerge at random intervals to dance on the granite paving, splashing and spattering to provide an audiovisual treat. Laid out against the grid, however, is the exciting Dragon Basin, an organic, serpent-like structure of dark granite containing reflective water.

The huge scale of these landscape features contrasts with the size of the square, which covers 1ha (2.5 acres). Gustafson also attempts to unite the various buildings that surround it, including the Cathedral of Saint Corbinien (1995), designed by Mario Botta, which rises like a huge boat above the pale-grey granite paving. The limes planted throughout the square will eventually introduce attractive variations of light and shade.

Above The gardens for Shell Petroleum's headquarters near Paris contrast subtle and sensuous land forms with sharp architectural detail. Monumental walls emerge from the gently folded lawns, which conceal an underground car park. The lawns provide a dramatic point of entry and run down to sparkling water alongside the wide path.

Above In this rose pergola in her garden at Terrasson-la-Villedieu, Gustafson mixes modern materials with romantic imagery. The steel structure sits in the hillside, creating a roof of colour and perfume, in a contemporary interpretation of a well-used theme. The steel supports create a rippling grid that is repeated in shadow patterns cast on the ground.

The sculptural forms of much of Gustafson's schemes make it necessary for her to use models to communicate her ideas most effectively. As well as being important to her and her team of designers, these three-dimensional explorations also enable her to explain complex forms to the contractors and the builders who construct the finished designs. Gustafson is currently working with the architect Neil Porter, a partnership that has enabled her practice to develop a true landscape-architectural role.

Her work is both popular with the public and admired by professionals. She regards this as a rewarding response and a justification for the consideration she gives to intuition, memory, and emotion in evolving her designs. While these qualities are difficult to teach or even to quantify, they are nevertheless undeniably present in her creations. Gustafson has been an inspiration to students of landscape and garden design who have graduated in recent years, and lights a path for those still to come.

Above Steele's garden at Naumkeag shows a variety of experimental spaces and ideas inspired by European modernism. The Birch Walk combines graceful silvered trunks with the almost maritime architectural detail of white balustrade and deep-blue alcoves. The curving flights of steps splay out gracefully into the light planting.

Fletcher Steele

While training as a landscape architect at Harvard from 1907–09, Fletcher Steele (1885–1971) would have been immersed in the Beaux-Arts tradition. At that time the accepted approach to design, this teaching was based on formal and symmetrical principles, applied in the grand manner. Its origins lay in the École des Beaux-Arts in Paris, which perpetuated the French design tradition of the seventeenth and eighteenth centuries. It was against this stifling system that Garrett Eckbo, James Rose, and Dan Kiley rebelled in the late 1930s.

Fletcher Steele was no rebel, but soon after he began to practice he realized that other approaches and philosophies were not only possible but indeed preferable to these most traditional ones. Eckbo was to describe him as "the transitional figure between the old guard and the moderns."

Traditionally, materials had been employed decoratively, and in this sense were subordinate to their application. By contrast, modernists selected materials for their appropriateness to their function. Steele effectively turned his training upside down and became a progressive designer, influencing many who followed in his footsteps. This legacy was in part due to his sensitivity to the landscapes within which he worked.

Steele's travels in Europe were the catalyst for this change. He saw himself as an artist as well as a designer and often described his work as akin to sculpture. This was an avant-garde approach that allowed him to sympathize and embrace the work of Gabriel Guevrekian and Paul and André Véra, whose gardens he saw and analyzed at the Paris Exposition of 1925. Almost immediately after this his work became more abstract and geometrically controlled, importing European thinking into the North American domain. Many consider this dissemination of information between designers to have been Steele's greatest contribution to the development of design thinking over the century.

His masterpiece is to be found at Naumkeag, Stockbridge, Massachusetts, a garden created for Mabel Choate around a house designed by Stanford White. The work includes a number of revolutionary and iconic design ideas. Steele used elements of the existing garden, created originally by Nathan Barrett, thus allowing the landscape to assume a mature quality. The introduction of new ideas into a ready-made framework is itself a modernist approach, but Steele went further by acknowledging the influence of the landscape that lay beyond the garden, using in particular the shape and form of Bear Mountain as a guiding idea. Later, he stated that this abstract sculpting of the land was the first example of the incorporation of background landscape into foreground detail to produce a unified design. It was also a precursor of the land art that rose in popularity later in the twentieth century.

The Birch Walk is the most abiding image from Naumkeag, suggesting Art Deco elements rather than those of any other style, but it is the garden's underlying sensitivity that will remain Steele's legacy.

Luis Barragán

Few architects have extended their vision into the external space of the garden. One is Luis Barragán (1902–88), who, in exploring and refining his own cultural background, created some of the most exhilarating gardens of the modern age.

Barragán manipulated surfaces to achieve stunning effects with the searing light of his native Mexico, contrasting coloured renders with dramatic shadows and reflective pools. He was a true modernist, but he also combined his sharply detailed architectural forms with the texture and patina of the Mexican landscape.

His most famous works are the San Cristóbal Stables and the Plaza y Fuente del Bebedero, both in Mexico City. In the former design, Barragán exploits colour, employing a code for the various surfaces, gateways, and entrances. The house and stables are arranged around a central pool with ramped textured stone paving and glowing walls of colour; one of these walls forms a water cascade, spewing into the still horse pool to disturb the reflective surface. The whole composition is set against buff sand, giving the effect of an elegant and understated oasis. The San Cristóbal Stables are part of the larger Los Clubes development, designed exclusively for residents interested in riding. Nearby is the smaller Fuente de los Amantes (Lovers' Fountain), originally containing sculptures of two lovers carved out of old wooden water troughs, the inspiration for Barragán's cascade.

The Plaza y Fuente del Bebedero is Barragán's most atmospheric composition, centred around a long, dark stone trough and surrounded by groves of whispering grey eucalyptus. The reflective water surface catches colour and light from a free-standing white wall set against the azure-blue walls that simultaneously enclose the space and expand it. The glowing white plane of the wall is home to dancing shadows cast from the almost translucent canopies of the eucalyptus trees that tower majestically above it.

In his own country, Barragán's work was not accepted until late in his career, although he had won international acclaim much earlier. His awareness of colour and skilled manipulation of light are glorious recurrent features of his projects, which continue to inspire today's designers.

Below The San Cristóbal Stables illustrate Barragán's most enduring ideas. These are simple spaces, glowing with light and colour, decorated with gushing water and textured sand – a sculpted environment for man and horse to share. A training in architecture enabled Barragán to create a complete spatial experience both inside and outside his designs.

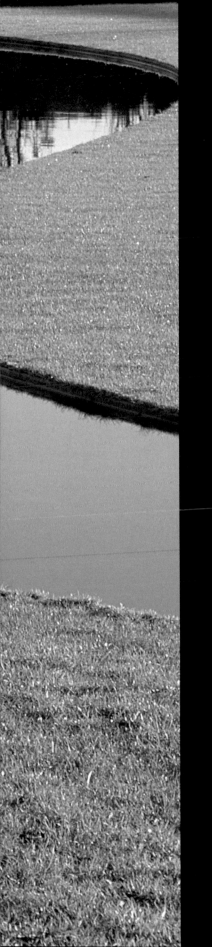

STRUCTURAL EMPHASIS

I n garden design the principles of two-dimensional geometry and three-dimensional form combine to produce the structure of the garden. A clearly defined geometry provides the basis for views and routes through the garden, and these are often reinforced by three-dimensional screening, illustrating the link between the two principles. The structure of the garden, seen through clearly defined geometry and form, contrasts with the irregular, organic shapes of plants. It is this crucial contrast that gives the successfully designed garden its energy and drama.

Above Harold Peto linked formal structure and informal planting in his gardens, pleasing the two schools of thought that together dominated the start of the twentieth century. His own garden, Iford Manor, Wiltshire, is atmospheric and full of architectural and planted structure. It stands as a testament to his understanding of scale and proportion.

Previous pages A section of the garden at Banque Générale du Luxembourg, designed by the Belgian Jacques Wirtz.

The traditional view of structure in the garden is linked to compartmentalization, the tight spaces and long controlled vistas typical of the Italian villas, and repeated so effectively in the famous examples of Sissinghurst or Hidcote and many of the commissions of Jekyll and Lutyens.

Harold Peto straddled the divide between the formal and the naturalistic schools of thought. It is often argued that William Robinson would have none of the formal in the garden, considering this approach an aberration. He did not argue against formal structure so much as against the formal use of plants, particularly those used for bedding. Certainly he removed yew hedges from his own garden at Gravetye Manor, East Sussex, though his great friend Gertrude Jekyll depended on their invaluable support. Peto seemed to befriend the

protagonists of both persuasions, creating rich borders and draping rambling climbers over formal, Italianate structure. What both sides agreed on was the quality of Robinson's highly structured work, often atmospheric and always romantic.

As the twentieth century developed and the Modern Movement's influence spread, structure opened up to imply control in a wider sense. Order and balance were achieved with asymmetry rather than symmetry, with carefully controlled geometry, and with a versatile and adaptable sense of scale or proportion. The axial and formal approach of the Beaux-Arts became another option, as opposed to *de rigueur*.

Rather than dictating the progress through the garden, the modernists favoured a much more abstract style, allowing the garden to be read or understood in many different ways. Screens were suggested or partial rather than complete, trees were used to create a sense of enclosure, both vertically and overhead, and the controlling geometry of the garden layout was used to reinforce the spatial qualities.

Although Thomas Church created many designs in his illustrious career, few have the power and energy of the El Novillero garden, completed in 1948 for Mr and Mrs Dewey Donnell. Perched on the side of the Sonoma Valley, California, looking out to the Pacific beyond, this garden has a structure that comes from the regular grid in decking and paving that underpins the entire design and from the sinuous curves of lawn and swimming pool that counter this regularity. While it is clear and decisive, the composition is also fluid and sensuous. The garden gives itself to the landscape in panorama beyond, with the existing mature oak trees providing one of the few hints of vertical structural definition.

With the garden at El Novillero, Church broke out of the straightjacket of the Beaux-Arts system, responding to the landscape with a freedom that confounded traditionalists and producing a huge leap forward in garden and landscape design. Although Church is often seen as a lone voice, isolated in California when most of the action was taking place on the east coast of the United States, he had links with Fletcher Steele, had travelled enough to see the organic work of Alvar Aalto in Finland, and was probably aware of developments in Brazil, where Roberto Burle Marx was creating a stir. There are echoes of each of these designers in Church's work, although the marked ability to synthesize was his own.

At Harvard, Dan Kiley, James Rose, and Garrett Eckbo rejected Beaux-Arts teaching and opened up the structure of their gardens and landscapes to the glories of space. Rose spent time in Japan and explored the structure of its traditional gardens, absorbing fundamental lessons in asymmetric balance into his work. This element remained in his passion for the private garden, even when Kiley and Eckbo began to move into the larger scale of public landscape. Sadly, much of Rose's domestic work has been lost.

Although Kiley bemoaned the dullness of Harvard's teaching of landscape history, he, more than any other modernist, has referred to the structural approaches of the past. Many of his designs have a classical quality, often based on an underlying grid, whose proportions lend his work a timeless balance and beauty. "In spite of his youthful rebellion, Kiley's mature work expresses a sense of historical rootedness and continuity that must be linked with the discipline he received from his Beaux-Arts teachers at Harvard," wrote William Howard Adams in *Grounds for Change: Major Gardens of the Twentieth Century.*

There are strong connections between the classical and the modern, and Kiley's work reflects this affinity. The Miller house, in Columbus, Indiana, provides the bridge. The use of the architectural grid of the house provided the basis for the garden's proportions, and it was on these that the spaces were then structured. The formality of the wide avenue, which focuses on Henry Moore's sculpture *Seated Woman*, is softened and made less formal by the use of honey locust trees to diffuse the light. Elsewhere in the garden, the severity of clipped hedges is broken by informal groupings of other trees.

Below Although Dan Kiley is more famous for creating public landscapes than private gardens, his work in both fields shows a clear understanding of structure and spatial definition. At Fountain Place, in Dallas, Texas, he uses a regular grid, together with dramatic level changes and elegant cypress trees, all on a scale appropriate to a large urban space.

This quality of the formal incised by the informal can be seen as a recurrent theme in Kiley's work, always structured through the combined qualities of powerful geometry and three-dimensional form. Russell Page followed a similar path, working from a modernist basis towards a more classically controlled system.

Page was to discover the historical background to garden-making late in his career. By then, badgered by powerful clients, he found it safer and easier to resort to precedent rather than to try to be inventive. Many of his European commissions came from rich or aristocratic families, living in historic or grand houses, and few of these were seeking the radical or revolutionary. For American designers the situation was very different, with such clients as Irwin Miller and Mr and Mrs Dewey Donnell keen to show a more progressive outlook. Ironically, this divide survives today, when many European designers are looking to the United States for more open-minded clients.

Page produced highly structured and detailed designs such as the Villa Silvio Pellico, in Italy, but his commission for the PepsiCo garden, near New York City, showed him capable of a much more fluid sense of spatial control, in which the planting matched the sculptures for excitement and drama. Here, there is a sense of spatial control contrasted with freedom, and this produces an exhilaration similar to that created by Kiley's work. Perhaps a different kind of client might have led Page to produce a different kind of result earlier in his career. Certainly, his other American work has a greater sense of freedom and more simplicity.

Sylvia Crowe, who came to prominence in the field of landscape design in the period following the Second World War, also utilized and promoted simplicity. Her structured approach translated modernist principles into planting design, and she will be remembered mainly for her famous book *Garden Design*. Crowe's work and her writing promoted the use of structural plants, those selected mainly for their form. This technique allowed the art of planting design to be developed alongside spatial and structural planning on the larger scale. Whereas many other modernists had left planting design out of their work, she resolutely pulled it back to centre stage. Her work for the Forestry Commission in Britain, in relating commercial production to respect for the value of landscape, was also ground-breaking.

The Belgian Jacques Wirtz brings a clear and refined structure to his work, returning to the use of hedges and compartments to define space, views, and spatial sequences. The contribution of the modern age is the simplicity and confidence with which he reduces his work to basic qualities of surface, whether ground plane or vertical.

The huge scale of many of his commissions plays a major role in defining their character, although the palette remains restricted, allowing the structural identity of the solutions to shine out. Wirtz feels that it is the "structure, readability, and the expressive strength of plant material" that mark his work out from that of others. Certainly, a homogeneity stems from the emphasis he places on the surfaces, but this quality also resides in the well-proportioned structure of the spaces he creates.

In the closing years of the twentieth century, Christopher Bradley-Hole returned to the modernist ethos of carefully structured but fluid spaces as a means of developing the art of the garden. His geometry is precise and combines symmetry and asymmetry in delightful measure, but light is encouraged to play on the minimal compositions, and structure is often just suggested in subtle and gentle ways. Peter Walker and Melanie Simo have written of *Invisible Gardens*, and Bradley-Hole, like Walker himself, has reduced the garden to a minimal quality, in which the essence of the design may still be found.

The structural plane is all the more important in these free and abstract spaces, promoting contemplation and maintaining the detachment that has always been so relevant to the concept of the garden. "The people who are making the important gardens today are those who are interested in the way the world is developing and are helping to shape its progress," Bradley-Hole proposes in his book *The Minimalist Garden*.

Below *The Virgil Garden*, shown at London's Chelsea Flower Show in 1997, propelled Christopher Bradley-Hole to fame as a garden designer and also revealed his background as an architect. The clean structure of the garden spaces was softened by planting in the New Perennial style. Plants, including iris, allium, and foeniculum, were all set into beds of limestone gravel.

Thomas Church

"Any tendency to design for design's sake, to create a pattern within which the owner must live according to rules set by the designer, is headed for frustration, if not disaster."

Thomas Church

The name of Thomas Church (1902–78) is synonymous with the Californian school of garden design. After studying landscape architecture at Berkeley, he graduated from Harvard in 1926, grounded in the Beaux-Arts tradition.

His early work was confined to modest suburban gardens in and around San Francisco, where steep slopes shaped his design approach by preventing him from relying too much on symmetry and formal arrangement. As the winner of a travelling scholarship, he studied garden and landscape design in France, Spain, and Italy in the

Left The gardens of the Bloedel Reserve, on Bainbridge Island, Washington, show the simplicity of geometry and structure explicit in the work of Thomas Church. Standing on the edge of the Pacific, they combine a wild and spiritual quality with a precisely coordinated design.

late 1920s, and found great similarities between these Mediterranean countries and California.

The Sullivan garden, in San Francisco, is remarkable for its use of a bold diagonal geometry that creates a dynamic sense of perspective as it cuts across the site. This technique echoed the work of André and Paul Véra and Gabriel Guevrekian in France, but Church also appeared able to accentuate length and increase the sense of space. In other gardens he had started to use timber decking, an appropriate material for the Californian slopes, together with the built-in benches that would be found in gardens later in the twentieth century.

As the Bauhaus influence started to permeate design circles in the mid-1930s, Church found himself drawn to Europe again. He became fascinated by Cubism and also met, in Finland, the

architect Alvar Aalto, whose work was much more organic and sensuous than that of the Bauhaus. These two influences seemed to set him on a completely new trajectory, transforming his work.

The concept of Cubism was applied by including in the design a range of important views rather than employing a fixed or central viewing position. This increases the dynamic of the garden, creating a sensation of movement and spatial complexity, based on asymmetry. The garden that illustrates this style is El Novillero, created by Church for Mr and Mrs Dewey Donnell in the Sonoma Valley, California, and seen by many as the icon of twentieth-century garden design.

Completed in 1948, this garden blends function, modern materials, Cubist theory, and sensitivity to location. It sits on the valley side, embracing the view of the marshes beyond, through which the river meanders in elegant curves. These soft lines are echoed in the swimming pool, sited on the main garden terrace, the last a regular grid of *in-situ* concrete, based on the architectural grid of the house. The contrast between this grid and the curves of the pool and lawns creates visual excitement through counterpoint. Adjoining the pool terrace are redwood decks, carefully arranged around the oaks already there, which spread their mature canopies across the garden, framing the view and decorating the ground with complex shadow patterns. The boundary between garden and landscape is almost non-existent, allowing the eye to run on to the distant Pacific. A sense of space is this garden's overwhelming and exhilarating characteristic.

In 1948 Church created a garden for a beach house at Aptos, south of San Francisco. This is a composition of deck, sand, and simple planting, again combining sinuous curves and a controlling grid. The design expressed its function as a space for leisure and pleasure in which gardening was not a central issue.

Church published his first book, *Gardens Are for People* – now considered a classic – in 1955. He writes almost as if in conversation with a client, looking at how they live their life, how best a garden might suit them, how much time they might have for gardening, and how they might bring their entertaining out of doors. Although nowadays we tend to take these considerations for granted, in the 1950s the idea that the garden could be used for anything other than plants was a huge departure from the accepted view of its role.

In many of the case studies that he includes in *Gardens Are for People*, Church not only explains how design solutions have been achieved but how topography might have affected the layout of a design. The tone is friendly, inviting the reader to understand his outlook on design and avoiding a dictatorial stance. In particular, Church acknowledged that the domestic scene was changing dramatically and that the garden was becoming smaller and more democratic. He was the first designer to remark on these changes in society and to address them for a wider clientele.

Many of Church's gardens use expansive areas of paving, partly for functional reasons and partly to reduce maintenance for the American middle classes. Paths rarely figure in his gardens, and, as a result, the whole ground plan is freed to allow hard and soft materials to flow together. This informality and ease expressed through a curvilinear geometry relates back to Aalto, who created a famous swimming pool for the Villa Mairea, Finland, in 1938; it perhaps also links to the work of Roberto Burle Marx, whose work in Brazil in the 1930s had probably been publicized.

Church produced more than two thousand commissions in his long and productive career as a garden designer and landscape architect. Not all of these exhibited the modernist principles for which Church is justly famous, for he was not a purist, preferring to listen to his clients and to work with them rather than against them. At the same time those gardens that allowed Church to explore modernism have lived on, making him one of the most revered designers of the twentieth century.

Left El Novillero is a classic twentieth-century garden, celebrating space, geometry, and form as essential characteristics. An underlying grid relates the garden to the residence, while sensuous curves imitate the meandering river and salt flats beyond. The existing oaks provide an essential frame, whereas the boundaries are almost invisible.

Russell Page

"My pre-occupation is with the relationships between objects, whether
I am dealing with woods, fields or water, rocks or trees, shrubs
and plants, or groups of plants."

Russell Page

Russell Page (1906–85) is regarded by many as the star of twentieth-century garden design, yet he always described himself modestly as a gardener. *The Education of a Gardener* (1962), his only book, is a testament to this philosophy.

Born in Lincolnshire, England, from an early age Page showed a deep interest in nature – something that remained with him throughout his life. He found pleasure in developing his parents' garden, transforming what was essentially a field into a structured sequence of spaces. An ardent admirer of Lawrence Johnston and his magnificent

garden at Hidcote Manor, Gloucestershire, Page was to refer to this time and again in his work.

School bored him, although he was interested in art and longed to learn about plants and their formative environments. At Charterhouse, Surrey, he won the Leach Prize for Art and went on to study painting at London's Slade School of Fine Art. By this time he had visited Gertrude Jekyll in her garden at Munstead Wood, not far from Charterhouse. He had also started to create gardens for others, and, gradually, the recommendations of family friends promoted him as a garden-maker.

Page had an ability to make good contacts. He spent time working in France, and met André de Vilmorin, from a family of seed merchants and horticulturists. This friendship would later prove valuable in professional terms. Amos Lawrence, an

Left The understated elegance of this glade at Kiluna Farm is typical of Page's work. The dogwoods and azaleas create a structural but soft backdrop to the sharply detailed, elliptical reflecting pool, drawing the eye into the open space.

Above The immaculate
parterre of box and santolina
framed by hedges at the Villa
Silvio Pellico offers a lasting
image of Page's approach. The
hidden cross-axis runs on either
side of the reflective pool, to
give the garden a much greater
sense of width than it would
otherwise have had. The
designer's attention to detail and
proportion relied on a clear
understanding of client and site.

Opposite The view up to
the Villa Silvio Pellico shows the
importance of the central axis
and the essential relationship of
garden to house. The massive
retaining walls extend the house
into the garden, creating a
strong sense of drama and
scale. Here, the formal
structure of this garden can
be easily appreciated.

American who was living just outside Paris, was another contact. Lawrence owned a library well stocked with books on design history, architecture, and garden-making in Europe. Page soaked up this information, and started to use the imagery and stylistic influences in his work.

It is difficult to know where his sympathies lay. He worked as a partner with Geoffrey Jellicoe just before the Second World War, when it seemed that modernism would rule, but the war put an end to the movement's potential. The short-lived practice had to close, and, tragically, many of Page's early papers, drawings, and notes were lost in the Blitz.

Just before the war Page had also met Henry Bath, heir to the Longleat estate, who enlisted his assistance with the layout of the gardens. This relationship would survive the war, and the consultancy continued into the 1950s. Yet another opportune meeting was with the respected French interior decorator Stéphane Boudin, when Page and Jellicoe were developing the garden at Ditchley Park, Oxfordshire. Boudin provided links to many of the clients with whom Page would work, particularly in France and other countries in the Mediterranean region.

In some ways, Page welcomed the Modern Movement in painting and design, but he was to shake off these beliefs on his journey through the classical landscapes of Europe. He delighted in their ancient cultures, developing an outlook that happened to mirror that of his clients.

Although the sites on which Page worked were undeniably splendid, the clean and free air of modernism was often hidden or overruled by the stifling blanket of tradition. To some extent this is a valid criticism of his work for the Festival of Britain in 1951, where a modern design that he developed with James Gardener was complicated by the fantasies of Osbert Lancaster and John Piper.

For some, this eclectic approach is the defining quality of Page's work. He could marry together the disparate elements that contribute to a garden's success. He was able to express the layout with great geometric simplicity, and to overlay his ground plan with stunning planting. Important structural elements were expressed in architectural hedging, and water, always handled with great skill and beautifully understated in primary shapes, provided a major focus.

There are gardens in which Page's true genius shines through and where he shows an impressive understanding of the site and its topography. His reconstruction of the gardens of the Villa Silvio Pellico, near Turin, Italy, is his most famous work. Dramatic terraces, simple box and santolina parterres, and the ever-present water all combine to create a spectacular experience.

Elsewhere, this magical touch of simplicity and genius seems to bless his commissions. The elliptical pool in his garden for Kiluna Farm, on Long Island, is pure elegance, yet it also has a dynamic quality that is complemented by the surrounding dogwoods, whose foliage and flower seem to float above low mounds of azaleas.

Winning commissions in Australia, Chile, India, and the United States, Page conquered the world. He could absorb information, critically analyze needs and functions, and decorate, all with equal passion and flair. His power to manipulate objects in space is perhaps best illustrated by his siting of forty sculptures on a 45ha (111 acres) garden at PepsiCo's headquarters, just outside New York City, creating a sublime and masterful composition.

Dan Kiley

"The thing that's important is not something called design; it's how you live, it's life itself. Design really comes from that. You cannot separate what you do from your life."

Dan Kiley

Dan Kiley (b.1912) is a truly celebrated landscape designer, an example to countless designers in the second half of the twentieth century and, at the age of ninety, still hard at work.

Kiley was born in Boston, Massachusetts, and feels fortunate to have been poor as a child, suggesting that this broadened his understanding. He enjoyed his sense of freedom but also subconsciously read the structure of his home territory. Part of this was the Arnold Arboretum, through which he would walk home from school. He was keenly aware of his environment and the

power of the landscape as a backdrop to his life, noting in detail the golf course where he caddied as a teenager or the woodlands that surrounded his grandmother's farm. The landscape was always a part of him, and in consequence his designs seem to be part of the landscape.

In the early 1930s, Kiley was offered a job by Warren Manning, then considered the top plantsman in America, for whom Fletcher Steele had also worked. Later, he enrolled as a special student at the Harvard Graduate School, while retaining his position in Manning's office. In this way he enjoyed some detachment from his studies and developed an independent outlook.

This became an important factor in the famous rebellion at Harvard in which Kiley, James Rose, and Garrett Eckbo reacted against the

Above The Miller residence set Kiley's career in motion. He linked the garden's ground plan to that of the house, creating a tangible sense of spatial unity. The honey-locust avenue, with trees planted into gravel, provides a focus. Henry Moore's *Seated Woman* gazes back to the distant bas-relief by Jacques Lipchitz at the opposite end.

drudgery of Beaux-Arts pattern-making by rote. Kiley feels that it was Eckbo who led the way into modernism, but the sense of release in exploring space and three-dimensional structure proved both welcome and timely for all three designers. Kiley left Harvard in 1938, without a degree but desperate to explore the field of landscape design.

In the early years of his career Kiley was introduced to Louis Kahn, a talented modern architect whose work Kiley considered to be inspired. They worked together on a number of schemes for the United States Housing Authority, and Kiley was to learn a lot from this experience. He also absorbed modern design principles, taking particular note of Margaret Goldsmith's *Designs for Outdoor Living*, published in 1942. Her principle of breaking down the barrier between indoor and outdoor space related closely to work that Kiley had carried out in 1941 at the Collier Residence, Virginia. In this garden, a series of terraces provided space for outdoor entertainment, and the "room outside" was effectively born.

During the Second World War, Kiley turned to architectural design before being drafted into the army. He was sent to Germany, where he was involved in the refurbishment of the palace at Nuremberg in preparation for the trials of Nazi war criminals. While travelling, he discovered the work of André Le Nôtre, whose clarity of line was to leave an indelible impression on him.

Later Kiley met the designer Eero Saarinen, with Kevin Roche, of the Miller house, in Columbus, Indiana. Saarinen invited Kiley to design the gardens, and he created what he regards as his finest work, "The Irwin Miller garden…it seems a miracle. I can't quite understand how I did it."

Architect, garden designer, and client were all thinking in the same way, an unusual convergence in any design commission. The geometry of the house, completed in 1955, is taken out into the landscape as a grid. The glass walls allowed this transition to be almost seamless, and the sense of space is exhilarating. The simplicity of treatment also contributes to the timeless elegance of the garden. Lawn, gravelled allées planted with gleditsia, and low decks of paving are separated by blocks of ground cover, allowing space and light to flow through the entire design. Borrowing from both modernist and classical themes, this abstract composition bridges the divide between the two to create a timeless work.

Forty years later, in the Kimmel residence, Connecticut, Kiley was still able to bring out these qualities of space and light, making the gardens emerge from and relate to the surrounding landscape. The main lawn is edged with a wide channel paved in slate to create a shining strip that reflects the broad sky. Kiley's work is characterized by an understatement that makes it belong to its site and compels other designers to say "of course." He manages to bridge the two disciplines of architecture and landscape design as a result of successful sythesis and sensitivity.

In addition to garden designs, Kiley is also noted for his handling of urban space, producing schemes such as the Henry Moore Sculpture Garden, in Kansas City, in which he explored the development of landscape design in relation to works of art. Fountain Place, in Dallas, is perhaps his most famous work, a celebration of water in the searing heat of Texas, in which pools planted with trees cover most of the urban plaza. Every day more than 2.4 million litres (635,000 US gallons) of water is pumped through the pools.

What comes across in both Kiley's gardens and his extensive writing is his great passion for the landscape, for people's interaction with their environment, and a sense that he feels privileged to have been involved in this work. His influence on other designers has been immense, both in the United States and around the world. Few designers have enjoyed a career as long as Kiley's, in which he has created work that in almost every respect represents the aspirations of the twentieth century. He is the acceptable face of modernism, able to create in spatial terms a voluptuous elegance that is both thrilling and sublime, when his fellow modernists seemed to have become obsessed with the international style and the horrors of greying concrete.

Kiley's designs remain as fresh and inspiring in the early twenty-first century as they did at the start of his career. He maintains that a design emerges as a concept from the nature of the problem set, after which the functions are analyzed and synthesized. This is pure modernism, and it underlines the difference between decorative pattern-making or stylistic interpretation and true design.

Above A dramatically reflective skin of water flows over dark stone paving to form the edge of the more formal gardens at the Kimmel residence. The sense of open yet structured space here is tremendous, and the wind-activated fountain creates an explosion of energy in a serene landscape full of light.

Jacques Wirtz

"When I am designing, my aim is to create tension and then gradually proceed into quiet."

Jacques Wirtz

Jacques Wirtz (b.1924) has been compared to various designers, from André Le Nôtre to Russell Page, but it is clear that he is very much his own man. He rejects the idea of stylistic classification, and says he draws inspiration from many areas, including music and fine art. Pursuing what some may see as an eclectic approach, he is happy to develop ideas from almost any source.

Wirtz's interest in music, particularly in Bach and Bruckner, brings to mind the peacefulness that pervades his work. Still, reflective pools, tall, clipped screening hedges, and smooth lawns create calm, timeless imagery in his commissions.

Within this carefully controlled structure graceful textures compete with bold foliage to create both counterpoint and excitement, crescendo and quietness. It is easy to relate the spatial and sequential control of his gardens to the movement and contrast in music. Grasses are often used in this way to soften the ground plan's sharp geometry.

Wirtz, who grew up in Antwerp, Belgium, studied horticulture and developed his interest in plants through maintenance work. He grew many of his own plants, and designed his first garden in 1949. His internationally renowned company continues to operate on a "design and build" basis, which allows control over both the design of a scheme and its implementation.

The Kontich Garden, near Antwerp, is classic Wirtz, in which he uses hornbeam as the main hedging plant, creating a series of enclosures. The

Left The tightly clipped hedges and topiary at Botermelle, in Belgium, typify Wirtz's highly structured approach. Hornbeam is often used as a structural element since it offers spatial enclosure with light-capturing transparency, against which more sculptural forms can be displayed.

hedges disguise the awkward shape of the site, and movement is encouraged along axial views. A long reflective canal provides a space for displaying tall, elegant reeds against water, lawn, and hedge.

The campus at Antwerp University and the Tuileries gardens, in Paris, are Wirtz's favourites of his works. The latter, which gave consistency to an important urban landscape, probably brought him greater fame. The same restricted palette of hedge, lawn, and immaculately detailed paving is used in both schemes, but the simplicity of concept in the Tuileries is bold and more than a match for the grand location, a site also linked with Le Nôtre.

Here the combination of radial hedge patterns, formal parterres, huge vistas, and the opportunity to link together the Arc du Carrousel with I.M Pei's pyramid at the Louvre has brought together many of Wirtz's favourite themes. He finds that being Belgian helps in his attitude to style and tradition, as French, British, and German influences flow through the history of the nation.

Wirtz feels that the structure provided by his hedges enables his gardens to work just as well in winter as in summer, a factor that sets them apart. Although he prefers to use a restricted planting palette, this decision hides a lifelong interest in and love for planting. His own nursery supports the design practice, and he is determined to retain his office in its rural location as this preserves his contact with the land and the planting that surrounds him. He suspects that many designers become divorced from their work, losing the contact with the landscape that plays such an important role in garden-making.

Recently Wirtz was commissioned to design a new garden at Alnwick Castle, Northumberland. Other work has taken him to the United States and Japan, often as the result of his winning a competition. This success perhaps stems from his designs using an international language.

Wirtz sees each garden as individual and for this reason he cannot see how his work could be categorized. A designer who responds to client briefs, personalities, locations, and his own inner reactions, he saw the 1960s as a period of change for the better, with increased freedom and self-expression that allowed the world of design to lose its stylistic inhibitions. For Wirtz the thought of interpreting his work and theorizing about it is tantamount to treason. He describes himself as a designer whose personality transforms incoming information, from whatever source, into the "calm, expressive, and homogeneous atmosphere" of his serene and spatially elegant gardens.

TEXTURE

The treatment of surfaces in the garden became one of the most expressive aspects of twentieth-century garden design. As space was simplified, and light came to be seen as an essential ingredient of the contemporary garden, so the surface quality of hard and soft elements grew in importance. Although the word "texture" refers to tactile experience, in planting design it also denotes the arrangement of foliage on the stem and often the stems, trunks, or leaves themselves. A number of designers use this potent design element to inform and define their work.

Above Roberto Burle Marx was a master manipulator of texture, a skill most often seen in his large-scale urban landscapes for Rio de Janeiro and Brasilia. In his own garden the textures of both hard and soft elements are also used to exciting effect, with almost every surface employed.

Opposite The use of grasses characterizes the work of Wolfgang Oehme and James van Sweden. Here *Miscanthus sinensis* 'Malepartus' illustrates its value in capturing light and movement within the border, as well as providing texture in leaf and flower for most of the year.

Previous pages La Florida, Madrid, Spain, designed by Fernando Caruncho.

As garden design developed over the twentieth century, an expanding view of the possibilities of the garden led designers to concentrate much more on surface qualities and the textures of the materials they used than before. Fine artists had already been exploring these qualities, and now architects and landscape designers adopted similar approachs. The results have been phenomenal, with light and shade playing as much a part in a garden's success as they have traditionally in sculpture.

Texture itself is clearly not a new idea, but the scale and format of the spaces in the enclosed and compartmentalized gardens that ushered in the twentieth century worked against the exploitation of surfaces and planting structure, save for limited experimentation in borders and terraces.

Roberto Burle Marx changed the face of garden design. Interestingly, he came into this field from an artistic background. He received training in which artists were taught architecture and

architects were invited to paint – a way of mixing skills and approaches that, in his case, paid off. It was therefore not difficult for him to progress from painting a mural for the new Ministry of Education and Health in Rio de Janeiro to designing the building's roof garden.

Burle Marx's name was made and he subsequently produced an extensive range of gardens and landscapes around a series of modern houses and government buildings. This work was carried out mainly in his native Brazil, particularly in Rio and the new national capital, Brasilia. Burle Marx did not paint with plants and hard materials, but he developed all of his designs with the eyes of an artist. His flatplans have the quality of paintings but they belie the three-dimensional qualities that typify his work.

His chosen plant materials, in particular, were richly textured, and Burle Marx applied these to his sites in huge swathes, drifting colour and patterns of light and shade across hundreds of square metres at a time. In some settings he would complement the architecture but in others he would outshine and overwhelm less significant structures by creating landscapes that were unashamedly the dominant force. In this way alone he revolutionized the role of the landscape or garden designer, often seen as subservient to the architect or architecture. For the most part, however, Brazil's Bauhaus-influenced architecture and Burle Marx's exotically textured landscapes proved to be very satisfactory companions. Burle Marx is one of the most influential designers of the twentieth century, and his penchant for large blocks, or drifts, of planting has been a particularly strong force in landscape and garden design in the second half of the period.

It has taken some time for this approach to spread to Europe and North America – a fact that has more to do with the reserve of clients than the inertia of garden and landscape designers, and a problem that still faces practitioners in these fields. Pietro Porcinai used texture but in a different manner, refined and precise, often employing simple combinations of paving with clipped forms of box or yew. The Italian tradition of shaping and

tightly manicuring evergreen and hedging species was taken into a more contemporary arena, linking with the work of Russell Page and, later in the century, with that of Jacques Wirtz.

In Britain, Anthony Paul took up Burle Marx's challenge with gardens that rely on the foliage texture of plants such as ligularia, petasites, and macleaya. Again, these plants are used in huge drifts or masses. "One needs to have swathes or great bunches of plants if they are to be prolific and work on the larger scale." Although moisture-loving plants provide the texture Paul needs in abundance, this does not limit his approach. A restricted palette is applied to all of his gardens, whether urban or rural, dry or damp. The textural interest remains in each case, often contrasted with timber decks and simple expanses of paving.

Paul is originally from New Zealand, a country of exuberant foliage textures and one undergoing dynamic progress in garden design, of

which Paul has been a part. This outsider's view of the European scene has helped him to present an alternative view, although he also has a high regard for Mien Ruys, who, like Sylvia Crowe, valued the textural and architectural qualities of plant material, as is evident in their plant associations.

The influence of Ruys also connects to Wolfgang Oehme and James van Sweden, two of the most successful designers of our time. This partnership's method is to fuse the American prairie with the best of contemporary European planting, including the "New Perennial" approach, to transform the character and atmosphere of the gardens on which they work. Like Paul, they mark a clear departure from lawns, hedges, axial views, and flower gardening into a more informal, textured, and naturalistic world, where spaces are defined by loose and luxuriant planting. These gardens are not imitations of nature but use and enhance the qualities that nature provides in the wider landscape. Using grasses as a mainstay of their planting palette, the two designers produce finely textured but mobile or dynamic planting groups, full of life and vitality for most of the year.

George Hargreaves works in a similar way, abstracting the essence of a place or location, but the results are very different. His garden for the Villa Zapu, in California's Napa Valley, reflects Burle Marx's methods, using the textures of mixed grasses to make a pattern on the landscape.

Shodo Suzuki combines the textures of hard and soft materials with seemingly equal emphasis. Bamboo verticals, simple ground cover, water, and textured paving create impact through contrasts and harmonies. His hard landscaping is often dramatically rugged or architectural, and the textured surface of gravel features prominently in many of his schemes. He manages to translate the Japanese garden idiom into a twentieth-century context, just as he captures the asymmetric balance, textural contrast, and reflective spirit that are the heart of the Japanese design approach.

Further around the Pacific Rim, Vladimir Sitta fuses a European background with Antipodean experience. As in the work of Isamu Noguchi, these cultural combinations produce interesting results. In Sitta's commissions an oriental quality expressed through texture is combined with an increasing sense of Australian identity.

Like Suzuki, Sitta uses hard and soft materials, often mixed with highly reflective water or mist. The sensory experience is taken further, with sound explored through echo chambers and fire, one of the most basic but essential elements. As in Burle Marx's work, Sitta's gardens show a leaning towards art, and many of them could reasonably be described as installations. He builds a rapport between client and location that produces gardens with a beguiling and atmospheric charm.

In Spain, Fernando Caruncho uses texture to emphasize a concept. His water gardens are purposely misted to increase reflections, and his wheat parterre in Catalonia links a new garden with its agrarian past. Carundo is one of the few designers to combine texture with formality, a controlled approach that sets his work apart from the more

naturalistic and informal direction of Oehme and van Sweden. Sitta and Caruncho are close in their use of texture but divided in their use of symmetry as a defining factor. Both create sublime landscapes that evoke memories and touch the senses.

What all these designers have in common is the search for simplification, as they pare down the design solution to the essence of the original idea. They show an increasing willingness to refine their work in order to clarify their response. Paul has become "more aware of over-designing. I hope I have become simpler and cleaner," while van Sweden is looking for a "savage quality, a roughness in the landscape that dissolves into the distance." Both designers will continue to depend on their eye for texture and make this element a defining feature of their work.

Below Vladimir Sitta uses objects and materials in a consciously naïve way, placing together a variety of forms and textures. His design details resemble his prolific sketches and his website in that all are full of fresh and unfettered thinking. In this garden, he mixes eroded stone, concrete, and fine grasses to produce maximum contrast and visual drama.

Roberto Burle Marx

"A garden is the result of an arrangement of natural materials according to aesthetic laws; interwoven throughout are the artist's outlook on life, his past experiences, his affections, his attempts, his mistakes and his successes."

Roberto Burle Marx

If one designer could be identified with the twentieth century, it would be Roberto Burle Marx (1909–94), whose work truly represents the modern era. His German father and Brazilian mother encouraged his creativity and awareness of music, art, and literature. It was his mother, working in a large garden that extended into forest near Copacabana Beach, who introduced him to gardening. In 1928 the family went to

Germany, and Burle Marx discovered the Dahlem Botanic Garden in Berlin, with its collection of rare Brazilian plants. Here, ironically, he came to appreciate the natural riches of his own country. On returning to Brazil he enrolled at the Escola Nacional de Belas Artes, in Rio de Janeiro, to study painting, architecture, and landscape design.

This mixture of disciplines was to stand Burle Marx in good stead, providing an opportunity to meet and work alongside the architects who would transform the landscape of Brazil. He was introduced to, among others, Oscar Niemeyer and Jorge Machado Moreira, who would contribute to the new modernist utopia of Brasilia and invited

Above At Copacabana Beach the lively, syncopated rhythms of Burle Marx's paving, a mosaic of small granite setts, create an impressive promenade. Many of his works are intended to be read from above, a design decision appropriate to the age of high-rise living.

Opposite The new city of Brasilia, which began to be built in the 1960s, provided Burle Marx with an almost blank canvas. Using water as a contrast to the heavily textured planting, he was able to produce stunning reflections, such as those that complete the drama of the city's Palazzo Itamarati façade.

Burle Marx to design the accompanying landscape. His knowledge of Brazilian plants was developed through his friendship with Henrique Lahmeyer, head of the zoological garden in Rio.

Burle Marx's most famous commissions were parks for high-profile sites in the public sector. In the 1950s Flamengo Park was created on a huge landfill site in Rio, containing a number of important civic buildings, including the Museu de Arte Moderno. Burle Marx manipulated the main spaces in a bold yet fluid way, using a geometric grid within which a wide range of planting types dominated. These, ranging from tall, majestic palms to waves of a variety of grasses, created a sense of rippling movement.

In 1970 these wave motifs were repeated in the gigantic promenade at Copacabana Beach, forming a pulsating pattern of syncopated rhythm along the entire promenade. Viewed from above, the design is spectacular, and its effect is further enlivened by the dancing shadows of the tall palms that line the edge of the beach.

Many of Burle Marx's commissions were designed to be viewed in this way, an innovation that offered a new perspective on the parterre for the twentieth century. Perhaps the most stunning example is the roof garden of the Safra Bank in São Paulo. This shows the clear influence of

Picasso, often expressed in the designer's abstract plan drawings and his use of hard materials.

Burle Marx's private gardens, by contrast, allow plant materials to dominate. The Odette Monteiro garden, near Rio, occupies a spectacular site, surrounded by dense forest and tall, brooding mountains. Colourful blocks of planting move across the main lawn in curving masses, offering changing arrangements as one passes through the space. For Burle Marx, garden design related closely to abstract art, and particularly important to him was the work of Picasso, Miró, and Arp.

In the Olivo Gomes garden, the house, by Rino Levi, sits on a high platform in a Corbusian manner, giving views down onto a reflective water pool, richly planted with mounds of textured foliage and serene discs of the giant water lily *Victoria amazonica*. Brazilian pines tower above the pool, providing graceful tracery in the mirror-like surface, beyond which the landscape opens to the misty distance.

A greater degree of intimacy is evident in Burle Marx's own garden, Santo Antonio da Bica, in which hard structural walls, mosaics, and textured paving compete with serene pools, sharp foliage contrasts, and ascending palms.

The gardens of Brasilia are powerfully expansive and sculptural expressions of their age. They needed to compete with the buildings of Oscar Niemeyer, around which they were created. The result is a staggering new city of concrete, water, and light. Burle Marx designed a garden for each of the ministries of Foreign Affairs, Justice, and the Army, bringing sculpture into their spaces. Water – a favourite element of his and important in this otherwise arid landscape – is used extensively to reflect the façades, sculptural forms, and mass planting, the last often huge strips or blocks of texture or colour.

Burle Marx's boldness and confidence with hard materials and planting has had a tremendous influence on the designers of the second half of the twentieth century, and will continue to be a source of inspiration for decades to come. Evident throughout his work is a single-minded pursuit of the bridge between art and landscape.

Wolfgang Oehme
and James van Sweden

"Curiosity brings us together. We have always looked beyond our own borders, both geographically and personally, opening our minds to learn how other people see and live."

Wolfgang Oehme and James van Sweden

From time to time a partnership facilitates more than the individuals would achieve alone. The work of Wolfgang Oehme (b.1930) and James van Sweden (b.1935) is the product of such a partnership, creating distinctive gardens and landscapes that are of America. The designers have become the leading proponents of what has been called the "New American Garden."

Both have links with Europe. Oehme, who was born in Chemnitz, Germany, grew up during the Second World War and lived through its terrible aftermath. After studying horticulture in

Bitterfeld, he moved into landscape architecture in Berlin, where the ornamental grasses used in the botanic gardens made a lasting impression. In German teaching of that period the influence of nurseryman Karl Foerster was much in evidence in the promotion of the importance of ecological principles and naturalistic associations.

Van Sweden was born in Grand Rapids, Michigan, and originally trained to be an architect. However, while designing a new town as a student, he realized that he was more fascinated by the space between the buildings than by the structures themselves. He went on to study planning at the University of Delft, in the Netherlands, and his experiences in Europe proved inspirational. In particular, he remembers the influence of Professor Jan Bijhouwer, who

Left The gardens of Oehme and van Sweden are filled with exuberant texture, often supplied by rolling, wind-blown grasses and finely detailed ground cover. Pathways chart routes through tactile planting, giving access to a rich tapestry of foliage.

Above A sense of discovery is an important feature of Oehme and van Sweden's work. In this garden for Barbara Woodward, sculptural elements are dwarfed by tall miscanthus or billowing panicum, to be revealed in early spring when the grasses are cut down to start their growth cycle again. In this way a dynamic environment acknowledging seasonal change is created.

Opposite Water provides the open space in many of the partnership's gardens, with lawn often diminished in importance or wholly absent, as in the Diamond garden, in Bedford, New York. The designers' gardens display their increasing awareness of ecological issues.

introduced him to Oehme. It was not until 1971 that van Sweden and Oehme realized that they could work together. As partners, they produced the van Sweden garden and established their practice on the basis of its success.

Their gardens were plant-orientated, with the lawn much reduced or entirely removed. The resulting texture is bold, and there are dominant planting forms and powerful masses with views and vistas caught between them. Van Sweden is particularly proud of the Diamond garden, a 14ha (35 acres) scheme devoid of any lawn.

The partners like to "think big, creating natural and relaxed landscapes using thousands of plants of one species rather than two or three of each." Van Sweden's own garden is designed in this way. He says that people find it difficult to restrict the palette of plants they use, so that the impact is often confused and lacking in structure.

Complementing van Sweden, Oehme brings a keen awareness of planting. Both have strong design ideas, but it is van Sweden who develops the early stages of a new scheme. He produces a master plan with another partner and deals with the client. Oehme then develops the planting concepts, and the design becomes a unified whole. "I bring architecture to landscape design and Wolfgang brings horticulture to landscape design …no one can know it all," van Sweden says.

During 2002 they were constructing a Second World War memorial garden in Washington DC, between the Lincoln and Washington memorials. Van Sweden sees the design, which took four and a half years to complete, as the pinnacle of their career.

A lasting influence is Mien Ruys, particularly her layered and expansive planting. Beth Chatto is cited for her ecological approach and massed textures. The partners' book *Gardening with Nature* (1997) is dedicated to Roberto Burle Marx, one of the most significant designers of the twentieth century, who shares with them a European rite of passage. All of these designers enhance texture in the garden, engaging in a communion with plants, and exploring the sensuous qualities of foliage.

The partners see their work progressing in an ecological and naturalistic direction, with more emphasis on tapestry-like meadows. Van Sweden has a new house and garden, developed in a more savage way. Near the house texture is emphasized (through perennial planting, including many native species), which fades into the distant flat landscape of Chesapeake Bay. Van Sweden acknowledges seasonal change as an essential attribute, and this is conveyed by the grasses, which remain into the winter, displaying their tawny, skeletal structure.

The German-American Friendship Garden in Washington DC embodies most clearly the partners' shared thinking. Built to commemorate the three-hundredth anniversary of German immigration to the United States, the garden uses the native plants of both countries, together with a clean, sharp use of water and paving. The cultural bridge between Europe and the United States is expressed and celebrated – a fitting tribute to an enduring and successful design partnership.

Anthony Paul

"I have always maintained that a strong backbone of geometry is the real key to all good garden design."

Anthony Paul

The inclusion of Anthony Paul (b.1945) in a chapter on texture seems appropriate when one considers his garden at Black and White Cottage. Dominated by reflective water, huge expanses of dramatic foliage planting, and tall trees, it is not what one anticipates in the English county of Surrey. And yet, the garden, which contains Paul's studio, feels both comfortable and energizing. There are few views out into the surrounding countryside, and the sense of escape is strong, so that the design takes on unique and magical qualities.

Born in New Zealand, Paul returns there regularly for commissions, as well as working all around the world. As a child he was responsible for tending the garden. By the age of twelve he was advising his mother on which plants would work best together. He recalls that he was constantly trying to change the quality of the garden. "What is the point of trying to change something – you might as well sit back and enjoy it."

His influences include Roberto Burle Marx and Russell Page for design, and Mien Ruys for planting. He sees the elegant simplicity preached by Page as an increasingly important goal in his own design work, where "what to take out" becomes the essential question. Paul's gardens are typified by decks – raised platforms from which one can gain views into the surrounding landscape or a different perspective within the garden. "I have always loved big decks that hang out, that you can sit on with great lush planting around."

Left The water terraces of the Koch garden use decks, sweeps of textured planting, and rough-hewn boulders as stepping stones to mirror the misty landscape of Lake Lucerne beyond. In combination these materials provide a visually dramatic foreground.

Above In Paul's own garden, which is home to the Hannah Peschar Gallery, sculpture vies with bold drifts of herbaceous foliage plants to create a changeable and dynamic landscape of texture and colour, form and mass. In this view the inscrutable heads of *The Committee* merge into the damp discs of the foliage of petasites.

Opposite Paul uses decks to slice through his planting drifts, bringing the viewer into close contact with the foliage but also providing elevated views over the textured planting areas. The effect is thrilling, and, because the decks often cantilever out over water or bog planting, dramatic level changes and dynamic perspectives occur.

These built forms find their counterpoint in dramatic planting. This is mainly herbaceous, as Paul uses shrubs only if he really has to. He loves the dynamic, energizing qualities of herbaceous plants, and their seasonal impact on the garden. He also uses sub-shrubs, with the result that his gardens remain soft even though the textures are dramatic. Against these larger plants he likes to set the finer vertical textures of irises and reeds.

Paul began to take a close interest in garden design in the early 1970s. He was passionate about plants and already had a background in fashion design. His idea was to merge the two disciplines by studying landscape design, and he embarked on a course at what is now the University of Greenwich, in London. He dropped out, however, finding it difficult to relate to the programme of study. Instead, he started to build gardens as a contractor, an apprenticeship that he found both fulfilling and an education in itself. He remains proud of his knowledge of construction that this practical grounding gave him.

Paul's gardens usually include water, one of his signature elements. While many other garden and landscape designers use water, he is exceptionally aware of how it can change the quality of a space. "Trying to use it without too much artifice is important. I try to make water look as if it was always there," he explains.

He also uses water as a means of linking the garden to the landscape beyond. This concept is evident in the garden he designed for Max Koch in Switzerland, in which the main water feature and swimming pool is set against the view of Lake Lucerne. Paul sees this as one of his definitive works; the image of the garden set against the mountainous backdrop stays with him. Similarly evocative is another current project, the Koru garden, in New Zealand, which is set against a rocky beach and a wide ocean view.

Paul admires the gardens of Ted Smyth for their simplicity. He also sees Thomas Church's El Novillero as a paradigm. It is simplicity that he himself strives for as his work matures and he becomes more aware of over-designing. Not surprisingly, these two examples are not in his adopted country. In New Zealand and the United States the absence of the clutter of history allows a free design spirit to emerge. The results are fresh and inventive, imaginative, even sexy, and Paul is happy to be part of that, stepping out of the more conservative client base of Britain. He sees a huge gap between the philosophy of British and western European garden-making and that of North America, but hopes that this situation will change. "In other parts of the world people break our so-called rules, and that is exciting to see."

Paul's planting runs in great swathes, and he has no hesitation in repeating masses of texture and colour. He sees no value in planting one or two hostas – great bunches or blocks are needed if one is to appreciate their textural quality. Ligularia, another of Paul's signature plants, sends shards of ebony into the air, topped with firework yellow. Massed in the damp earth around his studio, they illustrate his point well. Alongside the building a deck hangs over a sluggish stream, providing a glimpse of garden spaces beyond and a sense of involvement in the landscape. It is rewarding to see a designer effectively tasting his own medicine.

Vladimir Sitta

"I don't see the private garden as a place of naked confrontation and dispute with nature. Accessible beauty is still one of the elementary criteria shaping the concept."

Vladimir Sitta

Vladimir Sitta (b.1954) has his roots in Czechoslovakia, but it is his adopted country of Australia that has seen the flowering of his talents as a landscape architect. His remarkable designs combine dramatic gestures in stone and other hard materials with delicate planting tracery.

Sitta has displayed his renowned versatility by producing a series of large-scale estate gardens and a number of restricted urban courtyards in Sydney and the surrounding area. What he has brought to each of these commissions is a sense of drama – either restless and rugged, as in the Homestead Estate, New South Wales, or serene and surreal, as in the Smith garden in Sydney.

The designer is also famous for his drawings and sketches, prolifically produced to explore ideas and spatial concepts. His black-and-white drawings are cartoon-like, exploring sculptural forms within the landscape. Often on a massive scale, they are populated by tiny figures.

Three private gardens illustrate his approach, each one minimalist, with space and light the major players. The first is a tiny space, sometimes referred to as the "Theatre of Lights" because of its magical transformation after dark. The garden is paved with crushed green marble and planted with rows of bamboo, allowing the stems to form intricate tracery patterns across the walls and floor. Square black marble slabs sit above frosted glass, lit

Left In the Smith garden, Sitta plays with light and surface texture, using the bamboo *Phyllostachys nigra* to diffuse light and create shadow patterns. The use of slices of rock, arranged in parallel lines to span a pool of water, is a recurrent theme in a number of this designer's gardens.

Above The swimming pool of the Homestead Estate uses reflective water, mist, and river-like channels to create an intricate mixture of textures, ranging from smooth and sophisticated to rough and rustic. The ionized water emerges from a tall stone tower, refreshing and recycling the pool beneath it. The irregular edge of the paving reveals sharply detailed black mosaic below.

Opposite Sitta is a fount of ideas, producing beautifully worked pen-and-ink sketches from which emerge his imaginative and often startling gardens, landscapes, and follies. This installation considers the idea of natural growth, with foliage and plant forms emerging and disappearing around the graceful timber arc. Root systems protrude on the rear elevation to surprise the curious.

from below with fibre-optic lighting and constantly covered with a film of water, enhancing the depth of colour and creating a reflective surface. Mist is floated across the garden to create an ethereal effect, sometimes even making the ground disappear.

A rough granite slab, entitled *The Journey*, separates the marble slabs from the rest of the garden. The slab is divided by polished fissures into four sections, representing the stages of life. The main living room opens out onto the garden, with a wide limestone terrace providing a functional surface. After dark the space belongs to the interior, and there is a dramatic pattern of changing light.

Sitta's gardens for Bamboo Court, near Balmoral Beach, and Townhouse Court, on Sydney's North Shore, rely on patterns of shadow playing across horizontal and vertical hard surfaces. *Phyllostachys nigra*, black bamboo, one of his favourite plants, provides graceful patterns, and fine vertical rods of ebony swing in the breeze. In Bamboo Court Sitta plays with a series of bamboo rows, creating depth and ever-changing patterns, whereas in Townhouse Court the bamboo acts as a screen to the elegant canal of water, which contrasts with the terracotta paving of the main terrace. These two gardens both have disarmingly simple plans, but in each case the three-dimensional impact is richly rewarding.

Sitta's larger schemes explore more dramatic and complex concepts. In the Homestead Estate, New South Wales, local materials, planting, and the history of the location provide the narrative for the design. The main hard landscaping is close to the house, where a black mosaic channel runs like a river to the swimming pool.

Elsewhere in the garden alders have also been used to create a structure of interwoven branches and foliage that Sitta calls *The Green Cathedral*. Further out from the house itself, earth mounding and water open the garden to the wider landscape.

Two of Sitta's more recent gardens show that his imaginative mix of technology and nature has not dimmed. A garden in Sydney for Barbara Rook combines an Arts and Crafts house with a late twentieth-century garden. Lines of rock radiate like an explosion across the garden and include a sunken line of fire. The rock creates upstanding blade-like shapes across the neutral garden surface, with the flames copying the forms after dark – a brilliant and almost pagan feature.

By contrast, a scheme for a Sydney house designed by Adrian Snodgrass in the 1950s has produced a remarkable garden, linked to the building's redevelopment and modernization. The house stands diagonally on the site, and much of the garden relates to this trajectory. Water is an important connecting material throughout the site, although the quality of hard materials and detailing is also superb. A dramatic focus for the whole site is provided by the swimming pool, cantilevered out on a terrace to form a link with the harbour beyond. The pool is retained by glass, which creates a sharp infinity edge and gives swimmers a window on the harbour. From within the garden, the glass water wall provides a surreal textured plane set against the sky. On this project Sitta collaborated with the architect Luigi Rosselli.

Sitta has found his voice, and his work is increasingly sought after. His sketches reveal a boundless energy and an enquiring mind that leads him into uncharted realms of the imagination. Occasionally, these fantasies are realized, making Sitta one of the most exciting figures to take garden design forward in the new century.

Pietro Porcinai

Early in the twentieth century the designer Pietro Porcinai (1910–86) proved that a bridge could be built between modernism and the old world. Enthralled by the history all around him in great houses such as the Villa Gamberaia, in Tuscany, he found inspiration in his native landscape.

He was fortunate to be in Italy just as those with new-found wealth were buying old villas, farms, and large rural properties. These gardens needed an infusion of completely new ideas, and Porcinai, influenced greatly by Russell Page, found himself in great demand to redesign them.

Porcinai's work was distinguished by an eye for meticulous detailing and the use of bold geometry, both rectilinear and curvilinear, revealed in hedge lawn and stone paving. After studying agriculture in Florence he started to design gardens, creating asymmetrical compositions mainly using squares, oblongs, and rectangles. His geometry was always counterbalanced by planting, which he used three-dimensionally to create divisions, spaces, and maze-like patterns within his gardens. The results were particularly interesting as Porcinai worked as an architect, landscape architect, artist, and furniture designer – he was something of a Renaissance man.

Porcinai's most effective designs are spacious and well-proportioned, allowing light to define objects. He used sculpture and furniture carefully to emphasize particular locations or for the enhancement of the artifact itself. His garden for the Villa Riva, Saronno, designed by architects Belgiojoso, Peresutti, and Rogers, illustrated this technique well; here a mobile sculpture linked the old and new elements.

The Villa il Roseto, in Florence, is probably Porcinai's most famous work, incorporating a complex roof garden of arcing pathways, velvet-smooth lawn, and tightly clipped box. The deck is open to the city, with the dome of the cathedral creating a magnificent focal point. Beneath the garden is a grotto-like space, cool and mysterious, with light wells focusing on circular pools of water. This subterranean entrance presents a stark contrast to the light-filled garden terrace above.

Later in his career Porcinai collaborated with a number of other designers, notably Carlo Scarpa. Some of Porcinai's work is lost, but this prolific designer completed more than 1300 commissions. Throughout his life his influences remained the distinguished landscape architect Fritz Encke and the nurseryman Karl Foerster, two important German contributors to twentieth-century garden and landscape design.

Porcinai may have met and worked with Foerster, who was partly responsible for reasserting planting as a dominant element in the garden after early modernism had emphasized the architectural definition of space. In bringing together these various influences, Porcinai produced some of the finest twentieth-century gardens in Italy.

Below The labyrinthine patterns in the garden of the Villa il Roseto play with the textures of paving set against lawn and tightly clipped box. The restricted palette emphasizes the surface treatments, forming a series of interlocking circles. Part of the design incorporates a roof garden above a car park and a subterranean entrance.

George Hargreaves

The landscape architect George Hargreaves (b.1952) is most famous for his public schemes, with their elegant geometry and spaciously simple ground plans. Such a landscape is the San Jose Plaza Park in California, bisected by a low, crescent-shaped path adjoining a grid of fountains that emit a mist early in the morning and build up to a climax as the day passes. In this way the atmosphere and activity of the garden change daily from a mysterious beginning to a dynamic end.

Hargreaves responds to others and their needs, and in his public works he is interested in "connecting people to the larger environment." Where possible, he uses symbolism to link sites to their surroundings or history. In a similar way he develops his gardens by responding to the client's personality or the wit of the architecture.

This is particularly evident in the Villa Zapu, an outrageously decadent post-modern classic in California's Napa Valley. The villa, designed by Powell-Tuck, Connor & Orefelt, sits like a huge liner astride its site, and, with its separate guest tower, recalls Sissinghurst (*see p.19*). The garden is carved out of the surrounding native woodland to create a contrasting setting for the gleaming white architecture. A sequence of geometric surfaces marks out the progression through the site, from a circular entrance court, through a serpent-like arrival path, through the house, and finally to an elegant rectangular terrace above a dark, reflective swimming pool. This part of the garden is dominated by the tower, which serves as a guest annex. The structure is often draped with huge flags or banners that drift and unfurl in the breeze. Brightly lit and offering views across the countryside, it creates a sense of being adrift at sea in a wide, subordinate landscape.

The serpentine curves of the paths are picked up in rhythmic swathes of grasses that engulf the house, providing textured patterns to the entire site, emphasizing the form of the mound on which the tower sits, and creating wave-like shapes across the hilltop. The whole garden is sculptural – a syncopated pattern of surface quality forming an exotic clearing in otherwise dense undergrowth.

There are echoes of the work of Roberto Burle Marx in that the garden is visible mainly from above – a point that emphasizes the ground plan.

In the Dayton garden, Minnesota, Hargreaves placed sculptures with great care within a subtle landscape, reflecting the influence of Dan Kiley. Gently contoured lawns, finely boarded decks, and gravel walks create simple backdrops or surfaces on which the sculptures appear to dance or perform. Each piece is allowed to express its presence, with the particularly well-placed *Garden Arc* by Richard Serra forming a monumental crescent of dark, rusted steel.

Hargreaves is also noted for his teaching, and, as head of landscape architecture at Harvard, he has influenced a generation of talented designers who are carrying forward his references into the twenty-first century. He is a rare commodity: a successful academic who is fully able to put his theories into practice.

Above The exuberant architecture of the Villa Zapu is complemented by a bold and radical departure in textured landscape. Grasses create waves of life across the undulating landscape, providing a stark contrast with the sharp paving and ground plan of the house. This pattern in grass extends around the whole building.

Shodo Suzuki

Among the new generation of Japanese landscape
designers who use the rich cultural and spiritual
heritage of Japan as a starting point for modern
interpretation is Shodo Suzuki. Working in both
the East and the West, he creates powerful and
evocative gardens and landscapes, which are
unmistakably Japanese but which also depart from
his country's garden-making tradition.

Suzuki took advantage of the famous garden
festival held each year at Chaumont-sur-Loire,
France, in grounds designed by Jacques Wirtz. His
garden, *The Archipelago*, consisted of polished
granite "islands" set in a sea of raked white gravel,
reminiscent of Zen Buddhist temple gardens, such
as Ryoan-ji, in Kyoto, which presents a dry
landscape (*kare-sansui*) of raked quartz as its main
theme. The installation of granite rocks represents
the islands of Japan in a state of turmoil. The rocks
are disjointed, sawn through in precise fissures
intended to relate to the fault line on the edge of
which Japan is situated. The garden has a serene
quality and proved popular enough to survive for

most of the 1990s, whereas most of the festival's
gardens are retained for no more than three years.

The contrast between the polished stone
surfaces and the textured gravel is a recurrent
theme in Suzuki's work. He places great emphasis
on the juxtaposition of horizontal and vertical
elements, making his work firmly modernist. This
is particularly evident in his design for a garden in
Chichibu. The main focus of the design is a large,
asymmetrical terrace laid in horizontal bands of
stone that run out into the surrounding planting.
The vertical trunks of multi-stemmed stewartias
create the opposing contrast, emerging from
mounds of dense ground cover.

Water runs like a river through the centre of
the terrace, with large stepping stones allowing
safe crossing points. Elsewhere small courtyards are
decorated with gravel, moss, and vertical screens
to create retreats for contemplation that recall the
Japanese tradition yet are unashamedly geometric
and controlled. These themes are expressed in
Suzuki's sheltered, peaceful private gardens rather
than in his more exuberant commercial schemes.

Fernando Caruncho

Spanish-born Fernando Caruncho (b.1957) is among those garden designers who find inspiration in the rich heritage of garden-making in their own country. Towards the end of the twentieth century the garden world risked becoming a monoculture of English flower-filled gardens as a result of global media promotion of this style. Designers such as Caruncho, however, have developed a new spirit that combines innovation and pride in diversity.

Influenced by the structured approach of Russell Page, Caruncho has produced some of the most startling and evocative landscapes to emerge from Spain for some years. His gardens have a serene formality that relates to the historic influence of Islam, yet they are distinctly of the twentieth century: clean, uncluttered, expansive spaces full of light and reflective surfaces. Caruncho is not given to nostalgia, and draws inspiration from his study of philosophy.

From parts of the designer's S'Agaro garden, in Catalonia, there are views of the Mediterranean. A spectacular water parterre links house and sea, with a grid of stone paving seeming to float on the surface of the reflective pools. The water level is kept high against the paving, and fine jets of water spray the paved surfaces to create additional reflections and patterns of light. Pines surround the garden, casting dark shadows.

Perhaps even more dramatic is the enormous wheat parterre that Caruncho created for Mas de les Voltes, a farm estate in Catalonia. The whole garden relies on a formal grid pattern, but the wheat plantations are organized into huge rectangles, separated by closely clipped lawn allées, edged with cypresses and ancient, gnarled olives. Over the season the wheat changes in character, eventually becoming a golden sea of movement that glows with life and is punctuated only by the dark shadows of the cypresses.

Caruncho sees this garden as representing the countries surrounding the Mediterranean, which have been bountiful producers of food and wine since ancient times. Considerations such as this indicate a thoughtful designer, whose work is characterized by a growing assurance.

Below The extraordinary wheat parterre of Mas de les Voltes creates a dynamic tableau that reaches its climax in late summer and early autumn, when it becomes a waving golden landscape. The parterre is framed by tall spires of cypress and gnarled olives. Wide walks of emerald turf slice through the erect wheat, bringing garden and farm together.

MATERIALS

Every designer uses a palette of materials, but some adopt specific combinations that become a trademark, while others draw on a wide range of different sources with equal eloquence. Materials may be used to define a location, and Steve Martino's work, in particular, has a profound resonance of the desert landscape in which he works. Edwin Lutyens took great pride in using local stone and the skills of the craftsmen he employed, whereas Topher Delaney exploits modern technology to define her design concepts, with colourful and dynamic results.

Above The circle, or rotunda, seen here at Hestercombe, Somerset, was a favourite device of Edwin Lutyens. This example, executed in local stone, enabled awkward pathway junctions to be resolved without the use of over-complex detailing.

Previous pages A public land-art scheme that includes a series of stone monoliths, *City Boundary* in Arizona was designed by Steve Martino and Jody Pinto.

The twentieth century saw the introduction of new materials and technologies into mainstream architecture, few of which managed to escape into the more conservative world of the garden until recently. The Arts and Crafts Movement is partly responsible for this reserve, creating gardens that revelled in stone, lawn, pool, hedge, and border. These archetypal features, once they had been promoted by the media, coalesced into a template that took almost a century to change.

From the Arts and Crafts Movement emerged a remarkable talent, the architect Edwin Lutyens, who, initially more by luck than judgement, became the partner of Gertrude Jekyll, so forming the most famous partnership in the history of garden design. Like Jekyll, Lutyens was powerfully inspired by his surroundings during his formative years. Seemingly blessed with a photographic memory for detail, he drank in the vernacular architecture of the Surrey countryside.

His understanding and application of materials was always appropriate to the location. Sometimes this caused problems – for example, Marsh Court, Surrey, is built in soft local limestone, which tends to crumble – but the results were always justifiable in terms of architectural quality. Although there is an identifiable Lutyens style, the detailing was always fresh and differed from one house and garden to the next. In *Grounds for Change: Major Gardens of the Twentieth Century*, William Howard Adams wrote: "Lutyens's grasp of time honoured materials and building crafts, which he employed in his understated ensembles, reflected an original interpretation of vernacular traditions."

As the century progressed, the link with local materials changed. More efficient and effective transportation meant that a much wider range of materials was available, often imported from overseas. The evolution of modernism into the International Style also caused local character to be lost or ignored. Modernism at first was alert to local character, particularly in relation to the landscape, but it is only towards the close of the twentieth century that this characteristic was reunited with the modernist school of thought. Stephen Bourassa discusses the phenomenon of "critical regionalism" in his book *The Aesthetics of Landscape*. It is a development of post-modernism that "recognizes the importance of context…" and of "local culture, climate…topography and other elements of the regional context." The idea has been discussed and developed in architectural circles by such writers as Charles Jencks and Kenneth Frampton, but it also applies very well to garden and landscape design.

One of the designers who managed to encompass the qualities of modernism and critical regionalism was Frederick Gibberd, who reached a peak of success as an architect and planner after the Second World War. Although he was responsible for many buildings and landscapes, his own garden at Marsh Lane, near Harlow, Essex, is the outstanding testament to his feeling for locality. This relatively modest composition captures a true sense of place, mainly through its scale and its success in combining hard and soft materials. Here, Gibberd experimented with concrete particularly, but he also developed a sequence of spaces for the integration and display of sculpture.

John Brookes, one of the most influential of twentieth-century garden designers, has evolved as a modernist with a conscience. In his own garden at Denmans, West Sussex, originally the creation of Joyce Robinson, he marries textured plant material with gravel beds to form a dry-stream garden in the free-draining, gravelly soil of England's southern coastal plain. He borrows ideas from the local woods and meadows, encouraging plants to self-seed and find themselves a comfortable location. Many of his gardens combine this softly planted gravel with hard materials such as decking, brick-paved rectangles, and wide stone steps that hint at his modernist roots. Curiously, Brookes sees himself as "more Lutyens-like as he gets older in terms of scale, using broader and simpler shapes in a more abstracted way."

Preben Jakobsen works in a similar manner and sees no separation between the treatment of planting and hard materials. In his schemes, these two elements combine in ravishing associations of sharp brick or concrete paving, pebble-littered borders, and architecturally sculpted groups of planting. His gardens for Hounslow Civic Centre, in London are still regarded as classic designs, although, sadly, they have been a casualty of poor maintenance. Jakobsen's eye for the detailing of his selected hard materials is precise and always well researched. Jakobsen and Brookes are both designers with an excellent knowledge of horticulture, who have been able to transfer their skills into the successful detailing and integration of hard landscape.

Below Topher Delaney has an eye for simplicity, allowing the materials to speak for themselves. The Che garden, in San Francisco, relies for effect on green, textured wall planting and the drama of the water table, which is underlit to allow a sparkling circle of water to drop into the gravel beneath.

Above The various garden rooms of the Parc André Citroën, in Paris, provide clear images of Gilles Clément's approach, notably his manipulation of plant material for colour and texture. Rich planting is used to soften the architectural quality of the space, but the materials and the sense of openness are not compromised as a result.

The later decades of the twentieth century witnessed unprecedented creation of public parks in and around Paris, in schemes that involved both rejuvenation and new urban design on a huge scale. The Parc de la Villette, designed by Bernard Tschumi, became a flagship for the twenty-first century and the first in a series of major works. It was followed by the Parc André Citroën, which includes the work of Gilles Clément, whose sensitive handling of plants is matched by his bold use of hard materials. This architecturally restrained park, designed by Clément and the landscape architect Alain Provost, uses both planting and the structural hardscape to produce a dramatic landscape, a public playground for our times. Clément's planting is often stratified, layered horizontally and vertically, to reinforce a view or vista, producing a structured quality that suits the post-modern age. There is something inimitably French in both his restraint and his dependence on a structured technique.

Halfway across the world, in California, the work of Topher Delaney shares some of these qualities, notably in its emphasis on hard materials, which she explores and exploits with aplomb. She investigates her clients' background, dealing with memory and echoes from the past to create new landscapes of resonance. Hard materials play an important part in this process. Delaney is not afraid to exploit new technology and to use materials that have associations with architecture, engineering, and construction. Glass, stainless steel, and concrete repeatedly play a role in her gardens and landscapes, in many cases introducing colour, reflection, and light.

Delaney is especially fascinated by boundaries, and, like Thomas Church before her, she likes to involve the landscape that lies beyond when she is creating a garden. Some of her work is monumental in concept, defining spaces with walls of steel or glass arranged in ranks that recall the work of the American sculptor Richard Serra. Delaney often uses lighting to enhance these surfaces or to create an ethereal glow when it is seen through blocks of glass. This is a celebratory response to our age, with the designer delighting in the use of all available materials but revealing no hint of retrospection except in the interpretation of the past, aided by interviews with her clients.

Ludwig Gerns has a similar philosophy, using modern materials, including stainless or Cor-ten steel, alongside polished granite and rippling slate. The planting in association is precisely clipped to provide echoes of the past and a heady mix of influences. His work is sharply architectural and deconstructivist in quality, breaking axial views with "fault lines" that extend through paving and planting alike. The result is three-dimensional, producing mystery and surprise.

In Arizona, Steve Martino uses the materials of the desert to create fascinating and evocative gardens in an environmental response to a wasteful world. The arid architecture of the surrounding landscape is welcomed into his gardens rather than shunned or modified, lending them a sense of regional character within a modern framework of rendered walls, bold geometric forms, and textured gravels or sand. There is also a clear ecological message here, an appeal to conserve

rather than to waste, to sustain rather than to artificially maintain. The results respond to Stephen Bourassa's description of critical regionalism. Martino addresses this question with passion, producing eloquent landscape compositions.

All of these designers have created gardens with meaning, underpinning the message of their work, whether architectural and bold in the application of hard landscape, or organic and soft in the development of planting schemes. All are framed by the twentieth century, and reflect evolutionary steps in the use and application of materials in the garden. As the modern garden developed, so the choice of the right material became more and more important, either to reinforce regional qualities or to celebrate an expanse of colour or texture for its own sake. Finer detail and the adoption of new construction technology has allowed materials to be used more honestly and decoratively, producing radically different gardens from those of our predecessors. Once again, at the start of a new century, garden design is capable of mirroring the age.

Below The Stitler garden, in Phoenix, Arizona, shows Steve Martino at his best, relating the domestic space to the desert landscape beyond, in true modernist fashion. The reflective pool provides calm, reflective beauty amid seemingly arid and uncompromising textures. The sense of a boundary is intentionally lost through the use of rich, textured planting.

Edwin Lutyens

"A garden scheme should have a backbone — a central idea beautifully phrased."

Edwin Lutyens

E dwin Lutyens (1869–1944) is most often celebrated as an architect, but he was also a prolific garden designer, half of a famous partnership with Gertrude Jekyll. The gardens they created together came to symbolize the best of the Arts and Crafts Movement.

The two shared a passion for the Surrey countryside, observing closely its topography and vernacular architecture. Gifted with a photographic memory, Lutyens catalogued minute detail, which he later recalled on the drawing board. His drawings were beautiful, and throughout his career he relied on them as a visual record.

Left The garden at Hestercombe provided Lutyens and Jekyll with what was perhaps their most memorable commission. Wide lawns, deep herbaceous borders, and long planted rills open the garden to the gentle hills beyond, creating gracious terraces and the dramatic Great Plat.

Between 1893 and 1912 Lutyens and Jekyll produced seventy gardens, ushering in the twentieth century with some of the most elegant and atmospheric houses and gardens in the world. The historian Jane Brown refers to their designs as "gardens of a golden afternoon," created in a time of wealth, privilege, and leisure. The work of Lutyens and Jekyll typified what became known as the Surrey School, although in their case their work actually had its roots in that county.

The pair first worked together on Munstead Wood, Surrey, where the garden shows little architectural influence except for the more formal design of the North Court. This was Jekyll's house, her domain, and the planting spoke loudest. A neighbour, Julia Chance, admired the house and commissioned Orchards, one of the most important properties created by the partners.

Above The long pool at Folly Farm, Berkshire, indicates a growing sense of formality in Lutyens's work. A still, reflective pool with Italianate detailing, often enclosed by formal yew hedges, became something of a trademark of the architect, appearing in many of his gardens, whether or not they were collaborations with Jekyll.

Opposite Munstead Wood, Jekyll's own residence, was the first collaboration between Lutyens and Jekyll. The house was Lutyens's main contribution, although there were also limited opportunities for terraces, pools, and arbours close to the building. The planting was Jekyll's main interest. Most of the detail of the garden has been lost.

Lutyens learned much from Jekyll, not just about gardens but also about the layout of the house. Munstead Wood is a house and garden suited to an individual; Orchards represents a departure into matching the house to the location. The latter approach remained a trademark of Lutyens, who always planned that the main view would be enjoyed as one emerged from the house into the garden. It was to be repeated at Marsh Court, Hampshire, where the main lawn looks out over the valley of the River Test.

The Deanery, Berkshire, built entirely within a walled orchard, contains elements such as planted rills and domed water tanks that were repeated in several schemes, although perhaps to most spectacular effect in the garden at Hestercombe, Somerset. Jekyll would have inspired these details, which derive from her visits to Spain and Italy.

Bargate stone, local to Surrey, was used for many of the early houses and gardens. At Marsh

Court it was the local limestone that gave the house its distinct character. The sunken pool, again inspired by Jekyll, provides a dramatic focus in the garden, darkly reflecting the glow of the limestone by day and the light from the drawing-room windows at night. The white steps drop below the surface of the water, glowing mysteriously – a detail that Lutyens would repeat frequently.

As Lutyens's fame grew, he and Jekyll saw less and less of each other. Owing to her failing eyesight, Jekyll rarely travelled and would have seen few of the completed gardens. Having been sent the necessary information, she would design the planting accordingly.

In 1912, Lutyens sailed to India and over the next thirty years worked on the Viceregal Palace and gardens, New Delhi, now Rashtrapati Bhavan. The scale of this endeavour was enormous, and the garden remains a remarkable construction – a kind of water parterre with fountains, cascades, and huge planting beds set into emerald lawns.

The changing political climate in Britain, followed by the First World War, caused private commissions to dwindle. In 1917, Lutyens advised the Imperial War Graves Commission on cemeteries and memorials. The simple enclosures he created for the commission, lined with headstones and planted with many British native flowers and shrubs, are at once beautiful, haunting, and touching. He asked Jekyll to advise on the planting, convinced that cemeteries need not be gloomy. Other memorials, such as the Thiepval Arch, in the Somme, France, and the Cenotaph, in London's Whitehall, are also his.

After Jekyll's death in 1932, Lutyens continued to design gardens, but by now he was working in a much more classical manner. Two of his most notable late examples are his gardens at Gledstone, Yorkshire, and Tyringham, Buckinghamshire. As his career overlapped with the development of modernism, Lutyens expressed some concern at the lack of grammar and historical reference in the new approach. Nevertheless, when referring to the modernists, he admitted, in true Lutyens style, to a sense of excitement, finally asking why one should be traditional when one could be modern.

John Brookes

"…a garden is fundamentally a place for use by people. It is not a static picture created in plants…"

John Brookes

John Brookes (b.1933) is one of the most influential garden designers of the late twentieth century, famous for his work, his teaching, and his writing – the last bringing him international fame.

He grew up in County Durham, England, and came to love his native countryside, often helping on local farms as well as in his parents' garden, where his mother was responsible for flowers, and his father for vegetables. As he grew older, he became intensely aware of his local landscape, comparing it with the coast of Northumberland and North Wales, when his family went there to walk and enjoy contact with unspoilt countryside.

Left John Brookes became one of the most prolific designers of the late twentieth century, carrying out commissions throughout the world. The English Garden, in Chicago, is one of his favourites, combining a clear geometric layout with soft, informally structured planting.

Brookes's serious involvement in landscape design began after he had studied commercial horticulture at the Durham County School of Agriculture, and while he was serving a three-year apprenticeship with Nottingham's parks department. Here, he learned the practical aspects of horticulture but remembers the excitement he felt during the last six months of his training, spent in the office of a Dutch landscape architect. Suddenly he was inspired by the design process.

He sent drawings to Brenda Colvin, a successful garden and landscape designer and former president of the British Landscape Institute, who gave him a wonderful opportunity by employing him as her assistant. After completing his training in landscape design at University College London, Brookes went on to work for Sylvia Crowe. In doing so, he had managed to

Above Denmans, Brookes's own garden, gives him inspiration and a sense of spiritual renewal. This is essentially a gravel garden where much of the planting self-seeds, allowing Brookes to "selectively edit" the resultant associations. The effect is soft yet full of surprises, as in the walled garden, where digitalis stands tall among the permanent shrub structure.

learn from two of the most successful British landscape designers of the twentieth century.

A meeting with Geoffrey Jellicoe resulted in a recommendation that he should write and take a job as an editor for the journal *Architectural Design*. Brookes gained an insight into architecture as well as landscape, how buildings worked, and how fine art could be used as an influence on the design process. A series of his articles concerning the links between architecture and landscape were combined in his book *The Room Outside*. Published in 1969, this became a classic text for garden and landscape designers.

Enticing ideas were gleaned from Thomas Church, a huge influence on Brookes. Church

had sent his book, *Gardens Are for People*, to Sylvia Crowe – where Brookes saw it – and he remembers being impressed by Church's discussion of design, which indicated a new approach. The concepts embodied in this book were particularly revolutionary in a country where planting was considered the key element in garden design.

Church's book also struck Brookes visually, the simple line drawings emphasizing the geometry and form of the designs. He saw echoes in the work of then-contemporary artists such as Bridget Riley and Mark Rothko, whose influence crept into his work and his teaching. He taught first at Reading University, then at the Royal Botanic Gardens at Kew, before working at the Inchbald School of Design in London.

From 1964 Brookes developed his private practice, combining this role with teaching at Denmans, his home in West Sussex. The garden here was first developed by Joyce Robinson, an innovator who was deeply impressed by the gardens of the Mediterranean. She converted the smallholding into a gravel and dry-stream garden – a project that Brookes took over when he acquired Denmans and has since made his own. He cites this as one of the gardens that best represents him as a designer. The sweeping curves of the lawn have echoes of Church and his El Novillero garden (*see pp. 120–1*), although the gravel planting, relaxed and informally beautiful, still strikes a revolutionary note when compared with other English gardens.

Brookes's approach to garden design is still evolving in a number of ways. To some extent, the architectural quality of his planting is becoming more naturalistic, related to its location. In terms of pure design he feels that he has become closer to Lutyens as he has matured, aiming for broader, simpler shapes. He admires the sense of scale that Lutyens displayed and confesses that he aims for "purity and simplicity, increasing the sense of scale and simplifying everything down."

He most enjoys the design work on paper, working through his ideas both in concept and detail. The process of softening the structure of the garden – its basic geometry – with planting is particularly exciting, and he is still fascinated by

the way this matures on site. This quality of change is important to Brookes. Denmans is the only garden that he would constantly return to, yet this is constantly changing. He manages the garden through a process that he refers to as "selective editing," taking out self-seeders and invaders only if they threaten an association. He confesses to a quiet admiration for Kathryn Gustafson and Christopher Bradley-Hole, particularly for what he calls the "exploded formality" of their work.

The grid principle, explained in many of Brookes's books and still a mainstay of his teaching and design work, "keeps me on the straight and narrow." He finds it dynamic as an ice-breaker in the design process, allowing him to expand the dimensions taken from a building. It makes the elements relate proportionally throughout a site, and it proves especially successful with curves, giving a generosity to the completed garden.

Brookes seeks a sense of relaxation in a garden, a "dropping away" quality that seems to be at odds with a designer regarded by many as a modernist. He suggests that many new designers resort to the "shock factor, which works elsewhere but not in the UK."

In his writing, Brookes reflects on and carefully articulates his ideas, which then filter through to the drawing board. This he describes as the wider view, a thought process interrupted only by walks through his inspirational garden.

Above The combination of random planting groups and specimens with tightly clipped evergreens is a favourite device of Brookes, introducing refreshing contrasts into the garden and showing specimens to good effect. Here allium and onopordum are allowed to emerge through low ground cover beside the path, creating a more dynamic impact than the traditional border would allow.

Gilles Clément

"Gardening…demands a certain attitude. It is necessary to accept the dynamism of vegetation with serenity."

Gilles Clément

Gilles Clément (b.1943) made his name with his uncompromisingly modern designs for the Parc André Citroën in Paris, created with the landscape architect Alain Provost as part of the rejuvenation of Paris promoted by President Mitterrand. There is another face to Clément, however, a much softer side that belies his ardent modernism. He has a fascination with plants and the infinite possibilities of association, countering the criticism often levelled at modern designers that they prefer hard elements to soft.

After a conventional training at the École du Paysage in Versailles, Clément turned to private garden design – at that time an unusual move for a landscape architect. He was fascinated by the science of design and now teaches at Versailles and the École Nationale Supérieure du Paysage.

Clément's planting prowess is exemplified by his own garden, near Limoges. This is a relic of an agricultural landscape – soft, naturalistic, and lightly wooded – that he has enjoyed restoring. The design combines careful removal of undergrowth and the introduction of much more decorative and exotic material. The result is a controlled wilderness, a blend of soft native planting, dappled shade, and a large amount of architectural planting.

Away from this environment, Clément is much more structured, creating formal vistas, controlled planting, and harmonized hard and soft landscapes. The sense of space and the masterly use of materials demonstrate a crisp and confident

Left Gilles Clément is renowned for his planting design, but here shows great versatility in a Mediterranean garden that relies on bold colour and dark evergreens for sculptural effect. The brilliance of the colour contrasts with the pale limestone bathed in light.

potential. The property, now apartments, surrounds a long thin site, down which a thin carpet of lawn flows, linking the various levels as the site drops downhill. This green carpet ends in a dramatic pool, with steps descending into the cool water, decorated with dark boulders laid in strata.

The palette of materials is restricted to pale limestone, lawn, and foliage plants. While these all contribute to the classical French atmosphere, the design is undeniably of the late twentieth century. Mixing ideas in this way is typical of Clément's eclectic approach. Curiously, he admires the English garden, notably Sissinghurst and Hidcote. In both of these, there is a well-defined structure – a feature that repeatedly finds its way into his designs.

Clément has emerged as a champion of biodiversity, sustainability, and ecological prudence. In an attempt to convey the destructive force of overexploitation of natural resources, he designed the exhibition *Jardin Planétaire (Planetary Garden)*. This project, which combined design ideas and educational communication, was intended to show how we can continue to consume, exploit, and develop without exhausting the planet's resources.

This reflects Clément's ecological approach, in which he softens the often structured framework and relates his ideas to the locality. His work was acknowledged by the awarding in 1999 of the French Government's Prize for Landscape, given for outstanding services to landscape design. Particular mention was made of the enhancement and promotion of landscape design as an art form.

Geoffrey Jellicoe long hoped that landscape design would be the new art form for the twenty-first century, and, with the work of designers such as Clément, it seems that his wish is coming to pass. In Clément's designs there is a clear, imaginative, and expressive streak and, most important, a deep understanding of materials.

Clément remains a typically French designer, tending to restrict his work to his home country. France is a receptive community, interested in both the historical development of the garden and its contemporary manifestations. Clément has done more than most of his contemporaries to make the modern idiom a reality.

Above Among Clément's finest achievements is his work with Alain Provost in the Parc André Citroën, in Paris. The landscape incorporates French formalism, notably in the guise of themed planting and sharp construction detailing. Water, a recurrent theme, refreshes the sharp grid on which the park is designed.

Opposite The Parc André Citroën contains a sequence of garden rooms, each with a different planting character or colour theme. Here, exploiting both form and texture, Clément has created an atmospheric combination in which pine clipped into cloud shapes stands above smooth ground cover provided by box.

style. Clément seems able to control and structure planting to create informal associations organized within a formal framework.

The Parc André Citroën was developed where the Citroën car factory formerly stood, in an admirable transformation of exhausted industry into a revitalized urban landscape. Water features heavily in the design, with huge cascade walls and powerful jets playing in the light, and a series of distinct garden rooms. The Garden of Metamorphosis relies on a distinct and clear geometry for control, tied into the main structure of the park. By contrast, the Garden of Movement allows the planting to dominate in a wilder and more fluid celebration. These contrasts in texture and pattern work all through the park, changing the mood and developing fascinating sequences.

Clément's design for a town-house garden in Paris manipulates a restricted space to its full

Topher Delaney

"For Topher Delaney, this philosophical understanding of being in and of the world is explored through the process of creating gardens."

Maggie Peng

The designers of California have contributed significantly to the development of the garden throughout the twentieth century. Topher Delaney (b.1948) continues this tradition with her gardens that excite and stimulate the senses.

There is a profound sense of spirituality in Delaney's approach to design. She considers her discussions and interviews with clients as essential for gaining an understanding of their personalities and requirements. The results of this process combine art and science, sensitivity and shock, or subtlety and contrast. Delaney is particularly interested in the early years of a client's life, finding that memories of this time have a profound impact on preference, aspiration, and personal satisfaction.

The hard materials used in her schemes have colours that sparkle in the clear Californian light. Dyed concrete and tile in searing hues, stainless steel, slate, and textured gravel are typical, and these are coupled with planting selected for its sculptural or symbolic impact. Rarely cluttered, her gardens are often pared down to essentials.

Delaney is a dynamic individual, identifying strongly with her community and with social need. She has produced a number of healing gardens, often becoming involved in fund-raising as well. Having recovered from cancer, she has an empathy with those undergoing treatment or recovering from illness. She seeks to stimulate and involve patients in their immediate environment, considering such interaction as invaluable.

Left Clear, powerful colour is a recurrent theme for Delaney, from dyed concrete to kaleidoscopic mosaic. The intense blue in this roof garden creates a depth and purity, reflecting the sky and contrasting with the silver-white roofscape of San Francisco beyond.

Above Boundaries have a
special significance for Delaney.
In the Stamper garden,
California, huge blocks and
spheres of sculptural stone are
held precariously together to
form an obvious yet penetrable
barrier, between the cultivated
foreground and the wild
landscape beyond.

Opposite Delaney became
interested in design for
healing as a result of her own
experience of ill health. To this
hospital garden for children
she has brought life, vitality,
and colour, but the layout also
includes spaces screened to give
privacy and a sense of escape.

In her work Delaney always hopes to encounter a broad-minded view of the design process, pushing back restrictive thought, questioning accepted approaches, and seeking to break down the boundary between art and design. Growing up in an artistic family, she knew both the painter Jackson Pollock and Isamu Noguchi. Their work has influenced her own philosophy, as has the architectural control that characterizes Luis Barragán's work. Her training was in fine art, and its resonance is very evident in her designs.

Much of Delaney's work relates to boundaries, both physical and mental. In her gardens, there is a strong sense of the way in which the immediate space links into the wider landscape, and she is happy to watch them change and develop through seasons and years.

Often her gardens are precisely accentuated by vertical walls, sharp concrete beams, and grid paving patterns that acquire a sculptural significance reminiscent of Noguchi's work. Her garden in Greenwich, Connecticut, uses walls in concrete and stainless steel, partly to emphasize the topography, which undulates around the property.

Delaney simplifies many of her smaller gardens in order to achieve a sense of balance. The Che garden, in San Francisco, exemplifies this approach, using granite chippings as a clean canvas onto which a circular table of water drips its contents. The lighting is subtle, the planting is restricted to texture providers such as bamboo, and the fountain is constructed in black concrete. While the main impact of the garden is one of subtlety, there is no lack of depth and atmosphere.

Quite ready to take a humorous view of design, Delaney included colourful windsocks in one of her most famous installations, to express the windiness of the Bank of America roof garden in San Francisco. Another, entitled *Crossing the Boundary*, used mist to disguise the floor of a museum courtyard, providing a surreal experience for visitors as they did not know what lay beneath.

Delaney is dismissive of retrospective work. By contrast, the need to progress is evident in her work, and in the materials she chooses to adopt or adapt. Acknowledging that the cultural scene never stands still, she seems pleased to encourage others to move forward too.

Steve Martino

Steve Martino (b.1946) is one of a growing band of designers who are questioning their own roles and design philosophies. His approach echoes the revolt of Dan Kiley, Garrett Eckbo, and James Rose against the Beaux-Arts tradition in the 1930s, and like them he questions what has gone before.

A motorcycle accident that he suffered while training as an architect caused Martino to reflect. He began to work for a landscape architect and found external spatial design fascinating. But what appalled him was the limiting approach to the greening of the desert, which created landscapes lacking any effective relationship to their location.

Martino has opposed large-scale irrigation and the planting of exotics in the Arizona desert, favouring indigenous planting and construction that exploits light and shadow. The result is a series of designs expressive of their location, using beautifully textured desert plants, including cactus, agave, and acacia, set against colour-washed walls. Shadows are an essential element in these compositions, recalling the work of Luis Barragán.

Martino's ground surfaces are textured with gravel, which allows plants to self-seed under a watchful eye and also attracts a rich wildlife.

He has produced a number of private gardens in and around Phoenix, but in public schemes he involves the community, raising awareness of the environment, which many disregard through familiarity. *City Boundary*, a land-art project shared with Jody Pinto *(see pp.164–65)*, created a series of stone monoliths, now surrounded by native plants that members of the community helped to sow.

Water is often restricted as a precious resource, but in the Hawkinson garden it emerges from cool, shadowed recesses to splash its freshness into the sharp light and searing heat. The curving walls, which are reminiscent of *kivas* (traditional stone structures built by indigenous American Indians), disguise the awkward angles of the site boundary and introduce a new focus into this modest plot.

Martino has reconciled landscape design with the environment it serves. His approach departs from the mainstream, but many now see it as not just laudable but essential.

Ludwig Gerns

The gardener and landscape designer Ludwig Gerns (b.1948) has created a garden for his villa in Hanover, Germany, that represents the end of the twentieth century. The design is both eclectic and deconstructivist – a sequence of sharp, asymmetrical tableaux defined in hard and soft materials. For those who fret about the use of modern imagery alongside period architecture, a visit to this garden is a must. The house around which it has been designed is painted in cool white and grey shades to emphasize architectural detail and to provide a neutral backdrop to the dynamic garden.

The confidence with which the geometry is used to create the ground plan is refreshing, and a lively asymmetry pervades the entire design. This is not to say that the garden is informal, for the paving is so sharply defined, and the box and yew hedging and ground covers so tightly clipped, as to give a strong sense of formality. The two styles are played off throughout the garden, with precisely cut-and-polished granite standing side by side with irregular sandstone crazed paving. The rusted surface of Cor-ten steel is used to retain changes of level around the reflective pool, but glass and stainless steel form the boundary fence.

The overall impact is refreshing and exciting, but other influences can be glimpsed. Gerns acknowledges Russell Page and Roberto Burle Marx as his main design heroes, and the mixture of these two sources alone would explain much of what makes this garden so different. The use of a strong geometric ground pattern supported by clipped yew and box architecture provides echoes of both. Gerns also cites other sources as varied as Kandinsky, Le Corbusier, and Starck.

In the early years of the twenty-first century the impact of nineteenth and early twentieth-century figures such as Jekyll, Robinson, and Lutyens continues to diminish, but at the same time the legacy of the modernists is seen as increasingly important. In the work of Gerns there are certainly traces of designers such as André and Paul Véra, who made use of dramatic angles and asymmetry, as well as a revelry in geometry that he shares with Christopher Bradley-Hole.

The textures of both hard and soft materials make this garden work. It is essentially green, with highly structured paved surfaces giving dynamic contrast. The palette is restricted, but the impact is strong and clear, and the element of surprise plays a key role. Main axial views are sliced across with Kandinsky-like angles or crescents, or placed off-centre to create interesting imbalance, with sculptures providing the necessary focus. This sense of deconstructed ideas is truly of the moment.

Below The beauty of the Gerns garden lies partly in the quality of the workmanship, but also in the ongoing maintenance, which enables its sharp, uncompromising geometric forms to succeed. With its asymmetrical layout and formal features, this is a garden that allows formality and informality to collide.

Index

Author's acknowledgments

Firstly, I would like to thank my wife, Barbara, and my daughters, Rebecca and Naomi, who coped with the loss of a husband and a father for so many months in 2001. My second thank you goes to the designers and garden makers who have made this book possible, many of whom I corresponded with, or interviewed, and who always co-operated with good grace and a sense of

humour. My apologies to those for whom time proved too short for conversation and discussion. Writing a book whilst running two other careers was certainly interesting. I must also acknowledge the co-operation and support of staff at the Inchbald School of Design, in particular my secretary, Max Copoletta, the librarian, Richard Wallner, and the Principal, Mrs Jacqueline Duncan.

Photographic acknowledgments

The publishers would like to acknowledge and thank the following for their permission to use the photographs in this book.

Page 1 Nicola Browne; 2 Andrew Lawson Photography; 4 Clive Nichols Garden Pictures; 6 Garden Exposures Photo Library/Andrea Jones; 8 National Trust Photographic Library/Andrew Lawson; 10-12 Harpur Garden Library/Jerry Harpur; 13 National Trust Photographic Library/Nick Meers; 14-15 Country Life Picture Library; 16 courtesy of Hestercombe Gardens; 17 Photos Horticultural; 18 Garden Picture Library/Henk Dijkman; 19 Magnum Photos/Inge Morath; 20 Harpur Garden Library/Jerry Harpur; 21 National Trust Photographic Library/Andrew Lawson; 22 Garden Picture Library/Henk Dijkman; 23 Andrew Lawson Photography; 25 Garden Picture Library/Clive Nichols; 26 Harpur Garden Library/Jerry Harpur; 27 Andrew Lawson Photography; 28 l & r, 29 Harpur Garden Library/Jerry Harpur; 30 Elizabeth Whiting Associates; 31 Photos Horticultural; 32–36 Harpur Garden Library/Jerry Harpur; 37 Buro Mien Ruys; 38 Andrew Lawson Photography; 39 Harpur Garden Lbrary/Jerry Harpur; 40 Garden Picture Library/Marijke Heuff; 41 Elizabeth Whiting Associates; 42 Nicola Browne; 43 Garden Picture Library/Marijke Heuff; 44-45 Andrew Lawson Photography; 46 Harpur Garden Library/Jerry Harpur; 47 Harpur Garden Library/Marcus Harpur; 48 Harpur Garden Library/Jerry Harpur; 49-50 Clive Nichols Garden Pictures; 51-55 Nicola Browne; 56-60 Harpur Garden Library/Jerry Harpur; 62 Hugh Palmer; 63 Harpur Garden Library/Jerry Harpur; 64 Martha Schwartz, Inc; 65 Peter Walker and Partners; 66 Hugh Palmer; 67 Camera Press/Tara Heinemann; 68 British Architectural Library, RIBA, London/Sir Geoffrey Jellicoe; 69 Andrew Lawson Photography; 70 Nicola Browne; 71 Corbis Stockmarket/Nathan Benn; 72 Arcaid/Natalie Tepper; 73 Isamu Noguchi Foundation/Michio Noguchi; 74 Peter Walker and Partners/Pam Palmer; 75 Peter Walker and Partners; 76 Peter Walker and Partners/Hiko Mitani; 77 Peter Walker and Partners; 78 Nicola Browne; 79-80 Martha Schwartz, Inc; 81 Nicola Browne; 82 Harpur Garden Library/Jerry Harpur; 83 A E Bye; 84 Garden Matters Photographic Library; 85 a & b Charles Jencks; 86 Sofia Brignone; 88 View/Peter Cook; 89 Edifice/Gillian Darley; 90 Andrew Lawson Photography; 91 Nicola Browne; 92 Garden Matters Photographic Library; 93 AKG London/Tony Vaccaro; 94-5 Garden Matters Photographic Library; 96 Arcaid/Richard Bryant; 97 Yale University Library; 99 The Architects Journal;

100-1 Andrew Lawson Photography; 103 Andrew Wilson; 104 Nicola Browne; 105 Charles Hopkinson; 106-7 Nicola Browne; 108 by permission of Colvin & Moggridge; 109 Sofia Brignone; 110 Garden Matters Photographic Library; 111 Magnum Photos/Rene Burri; 112 Marianne Majerus; 114 Garden Picture Library/Christopher Gallagher; 115 Office of Dan Kiley; 116 Marianne Majerus; 117 Garden Picture Library/John Glover; 118 Harpur Garden Library/Jerry Harpur; 119 Enviromental Design Archives, University of California, Berkeley. Thomas Church Collection. Photo: Carolyn Caddes; 120 Garden Matters Photographic Library; 122 Curtice Taylor; 123 Helen Hogan; 124-5 Sofia Brignone; 126 Harpur Garden Library/Jerry Harpur; 127 Office of Dan Kiley; 128 Office of Dan Kiley/Dan Kiley; 129 Office of Dan Kiley/Aaron Kiley; 130 Marijke Heuff; 131 Courtesy of Alnwick Garden; 132 Marianne Majerus; 133 Marijke Heuff; 134 Andrew Lawson Photography; 135 Pieter Estersohn; 136 British Cement Association; 137 Andrew Wilson; 138 Fernando Caruncho & Asoc.; 140 Sue Cunningham Photographic; 141 Clive Nichols Garden Pictures/Clive Nichols; 142 Hargreaves Associates; 143 Vladimir Sitta/Terragram; 144 Garden Exposures Photo Library/Andrea Jones; 145 Corbis Stockmarket/Farrell Grehan; 146 Sue Cunningham Photographic; 147 Topham Picturepoint; 148 Clive Nichols Garden Pictures; 149 Oehme Van Sweden/Skip Brown; 150 Harpur Garden Library/Jerry Harpur; 151 Oehme & Van Sweden/Richard Felber; 152 Garden Picture Library/Ron Sutherland.; 153 Garden Picture Library/Ron Sutherland; 154 Clive Nichols Garden Pictures; 155 Garden Picture Library/Ron Sutherland; 156-7 Andrew Lawson Photography; 158-9 Vladimir Sitta/Terragram; 160 Sofia Brignone; 161 Elizabeth Whiting Associates; 162 Mise au Point/F. Didillon; 163 Fernando Caruncho & Asoc.; 164 Nicola Browne; 166-7 Harpur Garden Library/Jerry Harpur; 168 Nicola Browne; 169 Harpur Garden Library/Jerry Harpur; 170 Photos Horticultural; 171 Corbis Stockmarket/Bettmann; 172 Andrew Lawson Photography; 173 EMAP Gardening Picture Library; 174 John Brookes; 175 John Brookes/Apertures; 176 Harpur Garden Library/Jerry Harpur; 177 John Brookes; 178 Harpur Garden Library/Jerry Harpur; 179 Mise au Point/Arnaud Descat; 180 Edifice/Gillian Darley; 181 Nicola Browne; 182 Harpur Garden Library/Jerry Harpur; 183 Topher Delaney; 184-5 Harpur Garden Library/Jerry Harpur; 186 Vivian Russell; 187-8 Harpur Garden Library/Jerry Harpur; 189 Sofia Brignone.